NECESSARY ENDINGS

SOME THINGS NEED TO DIE FOR YOU TO LIVE

JUSTIN LESTER.

Dedication

To my Wife, Baby Cakes.
To my Son, Little Man.
To my Mom, Mommy.
Praise God from whom all blessings flow.

CONTENTS

FOREWARD
Rev. Dr. John Faison

————

My favorite book is *Celebration of Discipline* by Richard J.
Foster. It has been such a pivotal part of my spiritual formation, as it
translated spiritual disciplines into terms I could understand and apply.
Since 2008, I have reread this book every January. The more I read it, the
more one paragraph stands out for me. It is not merely a statement of the
value of spiritual disciplines; it is a recommendation of the kind of people
the world needs. Foster begins the first chapter with this statement:
"Superficiality is the curse of this age . . . The desperate need today is not
for a greater number of intelligent people, or gifted people, but for deep
people." This is a stinging indictment of our culture, our communities, and
unfortunately, even our churches. While we celebrate a surplus of
intelligence and giftedness, we suffer from a deficiency of depth.

Justin Lester is a graduate of Marquette University and Vanderbilt
Divinity School, as well as a doctoral student at Boston University. He is
both gifted preacher and budding scholar. Justin's passionate and
prophetic voice is quickly becoming a reliable and trust one in both church
leadership and academic spaces. He currently pastors the oldest Black
church in Rhode Island, Congdon Street Baptist Church. His masterful and
sensitive leadership has ushered Congdon Street through a season of
revitalization and into a rebirth of purpose and mission, proving that new

seeds can still grow in old gardens. Furthermore, Justin is an engaged community leader who is creatively impacting the city of Providence and the state of Rhode Island in ways that only time can fully measure. However, when I think of Justin Lester, I do not think of his intellect or his gifts. What comes to mind as a chief attribute is his depth.

Deep people, as Foster describes them, are not created in the halls of universities. Mentors alone do not shape them, nor do the experiences they accumulate solely develop them. Depth in the human heart is the product of a willingness to acknowledge, confront, and sojourn through the reality of one's own brokenness. These are not steps that shallowness can endure. These courageous steps require intense reflection and unrelenting honesty. These steps dispel pretention and resist duplicity at every turn. It is often a lonely, painful journey, but one that takes us from our knees to God's heart. In other words, the price of soul depth is costly; and the payments are due every day. The Justin Lester you will meet in this book is a man who has paid—and is still paying, the price to live a deep life. Moreover, he is wiling to share that journey with candor and authenticity. In our world, that is a gift for which all who read this book are indebted.

I met Justin during his time in Nashville, TN as a graduate student. Our interactions were brief, as he served at another church in our city. I remember him as a faithful staff member and team player. However, when he was called to pastor Congdon Street in 2016, Justin reached out. He was becoming a first-time pastor at a historic, traditional church, in a city where he had never lived, to love and lead people he had never known. If that was not enough, he was taking his wife, Courtney, on this brand new journey as well. That set of circumstances was not strange at all to me. In fact, it was eerily familiar. When I came to Nashville to lead Watson Grove Baptist Church, I left Virginia to become a first-time pastor of a historic, traditional church, in a city where I had never lived, to love and lead people I did not know. If that was not enough, I brought a wife and three children on my new journey. I can recall the uncertainty that we felt arriving into a brand new city. I can also recall the feeling of being the young, new leader of people who were often old enough to be my parents and grandparents. I vividly remember the cultural coldness that came with this new city. There were not many people, especially pastors, who reached out and welcomed me. So, almost immediately, we connected. I promised to be a resource to help with his transition, and to help he and his family in any way I could. I knew Justin and Courtney would need some friends. In fact, I knew they would need more than that. They would need safe space.

Before the end of 2016, Justin reached out to me on Instagram (that's how we millennial pastors often talk). He shared that God had led him to invite me to preach his first revival at Congdon Street in March 2017. I was floored and deeply honored. I know personally the weight of your first revival as a pastor in the Black Church tradition. Revivals in these spaces are not just simple services. They are moments of strategic significance. The right voice in those moments can empower and encourage a new pastor, while helping propel the congregation further towards God's desired future. On the other hand, a voice that does not handle this moment properly can disrupt what the new pastor is attempting to build, often delaying opportunities to fulfill God's vision for that church. Justin's trust of me to be that voice was not lost on me, especially considering that we did not know each other very well. As I boarded the flight to Providence, God impressed upon me that this was no coincidence. God was up to something.

The revival was an amazing experience! In person, it became very clear to me that God was already using Justin and Courtney in profound ways to impact Congdon Street and the Providence community. It also was very clear that they were navigating some leadership challenges through generational, cultural, and even spiritual divides within the church. Nevertheless, God never confirmed what God had said to me during my time at the church. God confirmed that something special was happening in another way. The highlight of the trip was being able to spend some time with Justin. Those three days allowed me to meet him, see him, and hear him. I did not just meet a young pastor leading a historic church. I got to meet a young man wrestling with his own personal narrative, sense of call and spiritual formation. I met a dude who loved the local church, but was also able to recognize the necessity of balance and the primacy of his family among the two. I met a guy who was so serious about loving his wife well that he was willing to acknowledge and confess his flaws publicly. I met a brother who loved Jesus immensely, enjoyed being Black deeply, and did both unapologetically. I met a soon-to-be father, who was looking forward to giving everything he had to love his new baby boy (Camden arrived in May 2017). God used that time together to carve out a space in my heart for Justin. Since that time, our families have connected on a deeper level. We pray for one another regularly. I have been able to witness some of their best moments, as well as pray with them through some of their worst. In every stage of our relationship, Justin has been willing to do the necessary work to live, love, and lead deeply. I am immeasurably proud of all that Justin is doing, but I am most proud of who he is becoming.

That is the space from which I write this foreword. This is why the insights in this book are so powerful. They are not the products of a shallow novice who is seeking to make a name for himself with a book. Conversely, these are the musings of a man who has committed himself to learning in the laboratory of life with God as his Teacher. When Justin talks about necessary endings such as "the death to feeling sorry for myself" or "the death to caring about they," he is not speaking as a casual observer. These words come from genuine experience, rooted in a vibrant relationship with the God Who helps us all with the personal funerals we need to have. The level of transparency with which this book is written was not something that had to be done. There are intimate, private moments that Justin could have withheld for the sake of his own comfort and reputation. Undoubtedly, there were some very well intentioned people who probably discouraged him from sharing so freely. Yet, that is not who Justin is. Because he operates from a deep place, he lives, and writes, as what Henri Nouwen would describe as a "wounded healer." We are made better because of it.

In John 20:20, Jesus appears to His disciples following His crucifixion and resurrection. In that verse, the New Living Translation says, "As He spoke, He showed them the wounds in His hands and His side. They were filled with joy when they saw the Lord." I have always wondered about this passage. If Jesus had the power to resurrect from the dead, surely He had the power to remove the evidence of His wounds. However, He did not choose to do that. Maybe He decided to keep them because He knew that the evidence of His suffering would lead to others being filled with joy. If Jesus could show His scars, it meant He had overcome them. I thank God for deep people like Justin who will show their wounds so that we can find joy in knowing ours can be overcome as well.

Rev. Dr. John R. Faison, Sr.
Senior Pastor, Watson Grove Baptist Church
Nashville, TN

INTRODUCTION

———————

Death was more than a thought. It was a wish. I attempted suicide in 2014 for the second time. The first was for attention in 2011; The second was to die. In 2014, I was a second-year master's student at a very rough time in my life. I was a leader in our Divinity School community, preaching everywhere, yet could not catch a break the way my friends were. I was frustrated with God, friendships, and finances.

Life was a mess. My father had stepped out of our father-son relationship to enter into a romantic relationship with another male. The father I had once relied on was no longer. In the direst time in my life, I was all alone. I knew I had to take matters into my own hands. Therefore, I sought out "father" figures to benefit my needs, but none of them were mine. My father was irreplaceable. Those other "fathers" had no stake, therefore did not invest in me the way I wished they would. Once again, I was left alone and without rescue.

One night at church, I was asked to lead worship, which made me feel important. I needed that! Through worship, I finally felt seen and heard. But in the blink of an eye, I found zero reasons to live. Once worship concluded, I was ignored and insulted by the same people who asked me to lead worship... Church leaders. That night I decided to end my misery by slitting my wrists. Not before writing a letter to my beloved girlfriend (now wife). I was desperate. I just wanted someone to see me, hear me, care for me, and love me. I hated everything about me. I had no reason to live.

I did it.

And then I woke up!

I was in a sea of Blood but alive. I was frustrated, but there was no doubt in mind that I was alive for a reason. I had a purpose. My attempt was gruesome and left a sour taste in my relationship with my girlfriend, but we pushed through. From that moment forward, I decided to live life fully. I realized that my attempts to end my life was in vain because I kept making it back alive. I was determined to find my purpose and live in it.

A few years down the road, and now I am a husband, a father, a pastor, and hold many other responsibilities. I realized that my life needed a concrete focus. This book comes out of that season of focus. Focus gives you a future and finality. When you focus on the future, you concentrate your energy on what matters while simultaneously delivering finality to what does not matter. Consider the areas of your life that need some finality and destruction. That's this entire book; Destroying what is against your future and giving it finality.

Growing up black in predominantly white communities, I shut up and played sports. I never attempted to explain my mental struggles and lack of well-being. Mental health was never something I shared with honesty. This book is an open door into my struggles, and an attempt to communicate and assist you to be all God has called you to be. I am alive today because I was ruthless with the word "No" and intentional with the word "Yes." "Yes," to whom God has called me to be.

This book brings to life all the hidden and unshared aspects of my life that have served as the foundation for how I think and interact. The language used is intentional and essential for the delivery of this message. I ask that you read with an open heart and mind. Whomever you are and whomever you are attempting to become, you are in for a life transformation. The entirety of this book speaks to the necessity to destroy what is against your future and giving it finality. Here you will find applications to walk away from your hindrance and walk into your purpose. You will learn how to rest more, save more in your finances, praise the Divine better, and become more intimate with your intentions. *Necessary Endings* will change your life. Don't let this book be a concept. Let it be purpose-full in your life.

Now, don't write this off as another self-help book with a sprinkle of Jesus. This book was born from a great deal of introspection and pain. Throughout my life, I have been told what matters instead of discerning what matters. Listening to the voice of the Divine, and triune, God has wholly rearranged and changed my life. Today, I can hold onto what God has prepared and, with delight, bury what I once thought was for me. After all, if God orders our steps, life's journey should be filled with joy! (Ps. 37:23). The expected is an organized, predestined mess like Calvary's cross. God does something beautiful with our worst messes. As we venture into the next few chapters and you begin to have some funerals, my prayer for you is that God will break the walls of the voices you believe are against you, the walls of your insecurity, and the walls built in your woundedness (Ps. 35:1, 91, 38:5). May the words in this book construct walls of peace and grace, so you can see exactly what God has in store for you.

Book Structure:

The first two chapters unpack the necessity for the death of what stands between you and your God-given destiny. To move forward, you must learn the importance of putting certain things to death. We will spend the latter half with the four necessary endings, concluding one chapter on "The Next Steps." I will share many stories, scripture, and principles I have learned that I hope will assist in wisdom building in your life. I want this to be an easy week-long read. A reference book you can revisit whenever you try to revive what is dead. Remember, you are destroying what is against your future and giving it finality.

Before coming to a close, I hope to not only encourage you but to make you aware of the inner authority you have to destroy anything against your destiny. You must know your life matters! I have cried too much for you to not hold on to your value. You are not here to live a mediocre life or a life already lived. You were created to live the life God has already designed for you. The world is waiting for complicated contributors to make life simple. This book simplifies your complications.

Now that we have simplified the chapters ahead, I want to welcome you to this journey officially. I believe life is an ever-evolving journey towards the full image of the Divine. Along the way, we leave and pick up some residue of God-meaning and making into our lives. Eventually, we can put some language into the God we serve. Consequently, we cannot begin something well if we are not able to end other things well. When we become willing to end things in our lives, we develop a deep engagement, a holistic fulfillment within our hearts' rhythm. Sometimes, our understanding may not come until it is time for us to go home... and I'm cool with that. Are you? Whether you are or not, this book is for you.

My understanding comes from various years in the academy and the world, as both a leader and a follower. I can quote an abounding set of people from Howard Thurman and Tertullian, all the way down to Kool Moe Dee and Nipsey Hustle. That's just me. I enjoy being me, living in my skin, and figuring things out. I have written this book the same way I talk and think on purpose. Through the raw nature of my life, I hope you can see your bare places and allow this work to smooth them out. My prayer is that you feel the tears and smell the literal bloodshed that made this happen throughout this work.

Are you ready?

Let's go!

I hope to enrich and end things with you.

I hope you are as happy as I am to read this.

I've prayed for you.

ENDING THOUGHTS:

What are you hoping to gain in your time in this book?
What are you hoping to learn about yourself?
What are you hoping to deepen your spiritual journey?

Take a moment and set a goal for what you will leave this book with.

Let's Talk!

CHAPTER ONE
Mountains and Funerals

I believe that we must lead from our stories. I am a 30-something, husband, father of one, and pastor. I pastor the oldest black church in my state. I also teach at a local university. With so much on my plate, life can get very unbalanced very quickly. My prayer life, work-life, personal life, and love life are essential aspects of who I am. When a long period of unbalance presents itself, it can create tension, but also health issues.

Since moving into a senior leadership position, I have had many health scares, mental breakdowns, and suicidal thoughts. Leadership is not a comfortable position to be in. Ronald Heifetz, author of *Leadership Without Easy Answers*, described leadership as, "Sitting on a Razor Edge."[1] Based on my experiences, I wholeheartedly agree. Nevertheless, in ministry, the impact of your work becomes enticing. When you become a witness to the fruit of your labor, you simply want to keep at it. This book was born from a "Keep at it!" moment in my life. I was on the verge of throwing in

---

[1] 1 Heifetz, R. *Leadership Without Easy Answers* (Kindle Location, 1542). Kindle Edition.

the leadership towel. In ministry and life, enthusiasm and energy can only provide so much fuel. Eventually, I understood the sickening mismanagement of my life. I could not continue living in a scarcity of time. Before things got good, they got worse. I wanted to quit my church, I wanted to give up on school, and I hoped someone would take my life away… because I was too much of a coward to repeat that scenario. I decided to take some time away within my uncertainty, which changed my life for the better.

Mountains

Every year I take two weeks away to a tiny home in the mountains of Vermont. I love it. I had a bottle of wine, a journal, and a computer with Netflix. Time away would do me good.

Once at my destination, I stepped outside and took in the calm, night sky. The stars were shining so bright I could almost touch them. The trees swayed delightfully, creating a beautiful melody. Without a doubt, nature's beauty slows everything into real-time. I walked to a nearby fire pit on the property with my journal in hand and sat down. I began as I usually do on these journeys, to set intentions. I looked out on the horizon and saw nothing. I cried. Even in the nothingness, God's beauty in nature was marvelous. With tears in my eyes, I wrote one statement:

"Something needs to die. This time it's not you."

For the first time, I had given myself a license to live. To live for my wife, for my son, for my God. I had to switch gears and completely overturn my mindset. My life has value. My future has a purpose. My old self could not continue to filter through my new me. I was led to scripture. I was led to sing. I was led to sit still in silence. Within this moment, I was able to live without the weight of others hovering over me. As I ended my time at the firepit, I watched an ember glow, and a scripture came to mind. Ecclesiastes 7:8, which says, *"The end of a matter is better than its beginning..."* My decision to live was certain. I crawled into my tiny mountain home and slept, utterly oblivious to the life-changing experience that was to come.

At 5:00 am on the dot, a rooster loudly and very proudly crowed. I woke up new, not refreshed, but new. As I sipped on my freshly brewed and scorching cup of coffee, I looked out the window and reminisced within the ashes of the fire pit. The statement, *"Something needs to die. This time it's not you"* was heavily on my mind and heart. I knew something had to be done. I quickly changed into my black t-shirt and black jeans. It was time to destroy and put to rest the sickening patterns of my way of thinking. On a mountain in Vermont, I held four funerals. They were not very well attended. There were a few squirrels, some ducks in a nearby river, and more than likely a bear somewhere.

In preparation for the funerals, I wrote down everything that kept me bound and distant from God and my family. My scribbles showcased my thoughts, some names, and stories. My tiny home looked like a crime investigation scene, with pieces of paper all laid out on the kitchen table. I could not have been happier. Slowly my life was detaching itself from the things holding me hostage. I began to write obituaries for each item. I outlined:

- All the ways I have hated and felt sorry for myself
- All of the "they's" in my life that I listened to
- All of my unfilled dreams that I hated myself for
- All of the plans I never fulfilled.

In the silence, it hurt. As I read the outline, I cried. I was upset. So much of my life had been lost to these things. It was disheartening, and I felt like giving up. But I had gotten this far, and there was no turning back. I wrote all of the obituaries, read them aloud, and watched them burn. The ashes of what was, were taken into the deep blue sky. In the history of what I mourned were dreams, notes, visions, and some phone numbers. It was not a "clean house" moment; it was a funeral. Through the death of what held me, hostage, I was able to commit to God. My emptiness could now be filled with God's love, grace, and purpose. It was a repositioning of whose I was. I performed externally, the freedom I felt on the inside. I killed it. I watched it die before me. Dreams, friendships, relationships, visions, and plans.

I held funerals. They were *Necessary Endings*. They were endings to mindsets and activities I could no longer bring along into my future. I was determined to become what and who I believe I could be. Why is that such a big deal? When you commit to ending some mindsets and thoughts you are deciding to deeply engage with the core of who you are, leaving behind what was to engage with what has yet to come intentionally.

I, Justin R. Lester, hate funerals. But, they access the heart of God in a uniquely and different way... One I seldom enjoy. Funerals always raise questions to me about theodicy. It makes me wrestle with who God is and God's word. While language and imagery around having funerals are stark, it is necessary. Funerals create the space to mourn with invested in the actuality and idea of who has been lost. In funerals, we remember, reflect, and sometimes even commit to completing the work of the person who has passed.

I believe everyone needs a moment like the one I had in the woods. A moment to destroy, kill, and put to rest all the dreams and visions we have created on our own and enter into the reality that God has designed. It is our responsibility to make room for God's movement among us. Through intention, we can actively enter into that movement. When we put those things to rest, we realize there is no need to pick up our pace or establish new relationships or "connections." If I am created to leave a legacy, then that is precisely what I will create. Legacy is not what you leave after death; it is the residue of God. Legacy is what you leave within, behind, and ahead of others everyday. Here are a few overarching principles I learned from these funerals. They will set the tone for the rest of our time together.

One Percent Better

The most oversized room in the entire world is the room for improvement. That room has to be big! In it lies opportunity and possibility. If that is excellence, then excellence isn't doing one thing 100 percent better, it's doing 100 things, 1 percent better. What a concept! The story is told of Wal-Mart founder Sam Walton who was a believer in details. One day he took his team to a local competitor and had them walk through the store. One of his executives looked at Mr. Walton and asked, "What are we doing here?" To which Mr. Walton replied, "I am here to put down our competitor, consider their customer service." Mr. Walton saw the creativity in their chaos and knew that creativity could give Wal-Mart a 1% edge over any competition. Meander through your life, what are the one, five, or twenty things you can do 1% better? Refuse to succumb to the pressure of the status quo, which itself means, "The mess we're in." Leave the messes of lack and dive into the opportunity to make meaning in your 1%.

Today well lived conquers tomorrow.

Today is the most beautiful day that continues to repeat itself. We live too often immersed in yesterday instead of capitalizing on the blessing called today. I am not advocating that we live coddled in a mindset distorted by sin. Instead, one of the most arrogant statements we can make is, "I'll see you tomorrow." Think about that. Ladled in that statement is the assumption that we will make it to tomorrow. We arrogantly lie between our teeth, that we will be able to finish tomorrow what we have started today. After scripture, I could quote scripture that offers insight on our needed humility, to number, and embrace our days. Yet, as I grow on this journey, I've realized to no longer put off important decisions and relationships for "Tomorrow." A day I like to call the busiest day of the year.

Think about it.
- When will you apply for the job? *Tomorrow*.
- When will you grab coffee? *Tomorrow*.
- When will you solidify the opportunity? *Tomorrow*.

Honestly, the real question is, when will you trust yourself? When will you Trust God? When will you listen to the notes to the song woven on your heart?

Tomorrow.

Why are we choosing tomorrow to handle the things we can do today? Simple, we are giving our strongholds power over us. We are not destroying, bulldozing, or killing the hindrance that stands between who we are and who God has called us to be. In layman's terms, we don't want the upgrade. We want to continue living in our *tomorrow* when God can reignite our dreams and spirit today.

Are You:
- -Financing someone else's dreams while you are suffering.
- -Celebrating someone else's ascension while you are the stepping stone.
- -Pretending interest in someone else's life while you are at home not living yours.

Do you believe that's the life God designed you to live? I do not believe that the God that I serve created me and you to fall into the traps of comparison and competition. I believe that God creatively and uniquely designed all of us to be just that. Creative and unique. It's time you start living your authentic self today, not *tomorrow*.

Desire Discomfort

Today is important because tomorrow is not a promise we all have. My grandmother used to tell me that tomorrow was not promised all the time! As a child I did not understand, but now I know. Knowing tomorrow may not come, is an uncomfortable reality to live by. But through this discomfort, we can grow. The places we are most uncomfortable are often the places where we can develop the most. Lean into and desire discomfort. Imagine taking all of your dreams, throwing them on the ground, and lighting them on fire. Now that is uncomfortable. When I finally put to rest all that was impeding my growth, I knew my today would be more significant and far more purposeful. Even Though it was gut-wrenching and painful, I was excited to share with my wife the new eye-opening vision for our family. My blank slate was set for God to begin to use.

There is a necessity to be wholly uncomfortable. Meaning, I was whole, focused, and painful at the same time. Discomfort brought a sense of peace and solace, something I had never experienced before. Yet, in my comfort, I had about myself. My dreams, plans, and relationships were keeping me from God. I had to quit being comfortable in narratives that I had in my head of self-depreciation and self-hatred and begin to own the true narratives (Phil. 4:1-10).

Comfort means we have overstayed our welcome. That is what opens the door for investment in your passions and priorities. A lack of investment in the right areas will cause us to be poor because of wasted energy. You cannot die here! Poverty is using everything you have in one season. Here is your help, end it! Get uncomfortable enough to end it. A lack of comfort will teach you full dependence on God. It is a corrective mechanism that will give the council where your passions will be deepened (Heb. 12). Within your discomfort, you'll be able to conquer all the places with your name on it. God has uniquely and creatively designed you to win within his parameters, therefore you are in a fight against yourself. Get uncomfortable and win. Allow God to drive out of you, pure happiness by teaching you humility in discomfort (Job. 5:17).

Your Journey is your Journey

The world is deadly afraid of people who are comfortable with being themselves. Nothing scares a world of insecure people more than people who are secure in themselves. As the embodiment of infinite possibilities, own your journey. Who you are, where you are, and where you are headed are for you. One of my favorite Bible stories is the story of the Prodigal son (Luk. 15:11-32). There are three main characters in the story, the father, the son who left, and the son who stayed at home. Jesus tells this story to inform us about the older brother and the impact Jesus has on the kingdom. The prodigal son leaves and eventually returns. The older brother assumes what the prodigal son did while he was gone, but we don't know what happened. Why? Because nothing mattered to the father. Not because the father didn't care, but because he was simply glad in his return. Whatever had happened was the son's business. The prodigal son's journey was his journey. It was his story. Own your journey. While it may be uncomfortable and different from others around you, your journey is your journey.

The mountains gave me the space to own me. That's why you're here. Own you. Don't apologize for being gifted and loved by God, own you. Continue the journey with me if you must. We are about to let some things burn, like Usher.

ENDING THOUGHTS:

What do you do for self care?
How are you, really?
What brings you Joy?

SCRIPTURES

Psalm 37:23 | Psalm 35:1 | Psalm 91 | Psalm 38:5

CHAPTER TWO
Justin and Jonah

_____

I do not consider myself a pastor, I consider myself a leader. I lead for a living. Leadership is not something that I was taught in seminary. I was taught how to be a great preacher and giver of pastoral care. I was never taught how to lead. Leadership hit me like a ton of bricks with balancing emotions, finances, management, and self-care. I never really gave up because I started to love the transformative nature of being a disciplined leader.

Throughout this work, I will reference scripture because I am a preacher by profession and call. Let me begin by unpacking one set of scripture that I want to share several different principles with you. One of my favorite stories in scripture, mainly because I relate so much to it, is Jonah's story. Jonah's story is replete with a call, follow-through, depression, anxiety, preaching, hatred, repentance and more. The best part is that there is no actual end to Jonah's story. It ends with an exposed prophet and an upset God. Let's begin our journey by unpacking a story with no end. Jonah's story is a picture of everyone's life. Continuously we are up and down, moving from one space to another, seeking to dive into the fullness of who we are. If you are you, no one else can compete with your possibility. End some things in your story, so God does not have to end it for you.

My Friend Jonah

As a kid, a family friend gave my family tickets to a basketball game. It was not just any game; it was a game versus Michael Jordan and the Chicago Bulls. This. Is. A. Big. Deal. We had two tickets on the floor and two tickets in a nosebleed section. Now, while Michael Jordan was a big deal, I was upset because my favorite player at the time was Charles Barkley. I arrived at the game angry and upset. I wanted to see Charles Barkley.

We got to the game, and I decided to go to the nosebleed section in protest. I had no desire to get close to Michael Jordan because he did not know how mad I was. My little sister, 4 years old, had courtside seats vs. Michael Jordan. These tickets were a gift for my birthday and I said "No" to the gift in my emotions and anger. I did not purchase or ask for these tickets, but I allowed my emotional distaste to devalue a gift I did not earn. As funny (and as much regret) as that was, think of the times you have done the same things with your gifts. God gifts you peace, love, joy, mercy, opportunity, grace, and we, in our anger, or pride, or jealousy, or arrogance look at that gift and tell God, "You could have done a better job."

Jonah is a minor prophet in the Bible with disputes on whether or not he existed. He could have been a contemporary of many of the minor prophets of his time, or Jonah could have been a superman story that prophets used as a story of encouragement. Regardless, here is my friend Jonah. And at the beginning of his book, like this one, God gives him a challenge.

Jonah 1:1-3: *The word of the Lord came to Jonah son of Amittai: "Go to the great city of Nineveh and preach against it, because its wickedness has come up before me." But Jonah ran away from the Lord and headed for Tarshish. He went down to Joppa, where he found a ship bound for that port. After paying the fare, he went aboard and sailed for Tarshish to flee from the Lord.*

Here's the story in a nutshell:
Jonah, get up from where you are.
Jonah, go to where God has called you.
Jonah, the place God has called you to is wicked.
Jonah, you are well equipped to do it.

Jonah is a great starting point for this discussion because, like many of us, Jonah did this to God with a story that does not get a clear ending because our story is continuing to be written. Jonah has this marvelous, wonderful gift to change the culture while internally screaming that he can do something better. Here are a few lessons from Jonah and Justin that prayerfully will reveal some growing edges in your mind as you pursue what God is calling you to do.

Get in a Rut

You are where you are today because of the choices you made yesterday. Tomorrow is a result of today's choices. One day, my family traveled to the northern part of Wisconsin for a family trip where there are two seasons, winter and July. As the back roads thaw, they become muddy, and the cars driving through it leave deep ruts. The ground freezes hard during the winter, and the highway ruts become a part of the traveling challenges. When you get to these areas, a big sign reads, "Driver, please choose carefully what rut you will drive in, because you will be in it for the next 20 miles." Your decisions are life-changing, kingdom shifting, and culture altering. Choose the paths carefully your life takes because once you choose, your choices will control you.

This proposition is scary to Jonah. Put yourself in Jonah's shoes. Imagine you mind your business, and you are selected to go and lead in a community that has never received a glowing Yelp review. Jonah's decision making was tested more than his calling was. Jonah's process of elimination and conflict resolution is called into action. Effective necessary endings are first a call for you to test your decision making and response to conflict, namely internal personal strife. Before you can be a multiplier of leaders and people globally, you must first tame your decision making personally. The most outstanding leaders are the ones who can make decisions under immense pressure.

Consider your decision-making processes:
- Who do you consult to help make decisions? Why?
- What do you read to help make decisions? Why?

Our reflexes are thermometer that reveals our internal pressures. How you react in your instinct shows what you really think about yourself and how you will engage with others. Consider your reflexes and who you invite to mature those actions. Be mindful of the positive and negative influences that kern your thinking, feeling, and doing.

Take the Second Step

This whole Jonah story is crazy right? God sees where Jonah is and called him to go to a place Jonah does not want to go because God knew what Jonah was capable of. Jonah can change the entire culture. Get the picture. Jonah wakes up, grabs his belongings and heads down to Joppa. Jonah had the resources needed for travel and left his hometown. Jonah took the first step with God. Do not mistake the necessity to take the first step! You cannot take a second step without taking the first step. Take first steps and action on a goal, but you must take the second step once you take the first step. Get past the first step. Salvation is built on not just taking the first step, but taking multiple steps.

One day I was talking to a few young pastors about pastoral ministry and vision casting. They were too determined to be great visionaries. Halfway through my discussion, I paused the conversation and said, "How many of you want to be great visionaries?" A flurry of hands shot up in the air. I responded, "Great, in that case stop this discussion on becoming a visionary, get your computers out and write the visions for your ministries." I packed my computer up, put some music on, and waited to see how many pastors engaged in writing. First steps, like having a discussion are significant. Second steps, like writing visions are what make the first step worth it. You cannot catch a fish unless you put a line out in the water. Take the second step. I want you to rejoice that you take the first step, but there must be a second step after the first step. The world and culture we live in caters to the first steps. Success is not in the first step, it's in the second step! Consider the areas of your life where you have taken first steps. Now, where do you need to take the second step?

Name and Say "No" to the Tarshish Dream

Jonah decides to travel to Tarshish. For the people in Jonah's day, going to Tarshish was like traveling to the other side of the world. It is a costly ticket and a long journey. Jonah took the first step, gathered what he had, ran to Joppa and decided that his next step would be a step in the direction against God. While God's word initiated jonah's journey, he decided to go the opposite direction. Jonah heads to Joppa in an act of obedience but chooses the destination Tarshish.

What was Tarshish? Tarshish was an exotic religious land, so much more exciting than Nineveh. Nineveh had a wrong and terrible history. Going to Nineveh was not a coveted assignment for a Hebrew prophet, but Tarshish was. Tarshish was exotic. Tarshish had an adventure. Tarshish had the appeal of the unknown. Tarshish was known to be an idealized port for people and a place of exotic escapism. In other words, Tarshish was a comfortable place to dream compared to Nineveh. It is easy to dream about what we've heard without experience. Consider your daydreams and dreamscapes. Dreams are great, but never forget that you are equipped to make each dream a reality. How often are you like Jonah spending time dreaming about Tarshish without facing the reality of Nineveh? Reality does not destroy dreams, reality shows you the necessary steps to fulfill God's dream.

You cannot seem to concentrate on your job because you are daydreaming about the next one. The same goes for relationships and friendships. In time you cannot stand even considering what God has called you to because you cannot keep your mind off Tarshish. So much so, you have convinced yourself that if you do not get to Tarshish you will not be a prophet anymore.

Before you destroy your dreams, Jonah's dreams of Tarshish were rooted in unhealthy values. Our thinking produces attitudes resulting in values reflected in our personality. How we daydream is rooted in what we value. We speak through our values in what we purchase, wear, and even our facial expressions. Jonah valued escaping, exoticism, and popularity. Defining your values is not just an academic exercise, instead it is a down to earth step towards fulfilling the calling on your life. Clear values are the first steps before your first step.

Here are some ways to clarify values:
- What do I believe in?
- What guiding principles am I obsessed with?
- What do I stand for?
- What puts meaning into my life?

This is not a simple one-day exercise because values are not made up in the spur of a moment. For example, I stand on four principles: Being Faithful, Consistent, Intentional, and Passionate. In every engagement and opportunity for my life, I ask myself if this will cause me to deviate from my core? If so it is not pursued. Jonah took a second step in the wrong direction because his values made his decisions. When you have exact values 99% of your choices are already made. Your convictions, not others, will determine how you live. Your value is the sum of what you value.

Consider this:

- What dreams are you trying to force God to make come true that you need to destroy?
- What decisions (good/bad) do your value system make for you?

Who's face are you looking at?

Jonah knew what he was doing. Jonah ran to Joppa and decided at that moment to be greedy, ego-driven, and in a real sense, he chose to be God. He knew that he was not only running from Nineveh he was running from God's presence. Why would anyone flee from the presence of the Lord? The presence of God is a beautiful place. The Hebrew word for the "presence" in this text is *"panim" or "paneh"* which is "face." It is a powerful metaphorical word. Think about an infant. Infants learn emotions by watching their parent's faces. Thus, the face is a space where we learn emotions and intimacy. The presence of God is where we develop what it means to be present with God and intimate with God. Jonah runs from God's adoration and Christ's commitment to stare at his ego and narcissism. It's a powerful thing to get a taste of God's face and desire *not* to want it again. When you flee the face of God you are running into a world that will affirm what you are, not who God is. How many times have you spent time seeking affirmation on you, not the God in you? This is a challenge of your prayer and praise life. Prayer is our response to God's constant invitation to be close to Him. God is continually trying to interact with us, how are you interacting with God? Prayer is both the easiest and most challenging thing we can do. It is easy in that God continually invites us to connect with him anywhere and anytime. It is also tricky because it requires radical dependence on God, faith that God loves us, and trust that God will show up. Prayer is hard work. Prayer is face work. Don't run from it, run to it.

Be Aware and Beware of your Assumptions

Jonah's gift was so cheap that traveling across the world, a much longer journey on a dream, was more tantalizing than traveling for three days to the exact place God told him to travel. His gift was so cheap that he used more resources to say "No" than the same resources to say "Yes." Jonah assumed that his ability was not strong enough to go to Nineveh, but thought it could handle Tarshish. God would not have called you to Nineveh if he had not equipped you and prepared Nineveh for your presence. Value who you are because you are valuable! What assumptions do you have about the places you live and work and how does that play into how you restrict your gift from working? My gift is good enough for my to-do list, but not for my friends. How many times have you cheapened your gift to handle Tarshish instead of testing it in and heading to Nineveh?

Have you ever noticed that we do not stress over the things that matter, but it's the things that do not matter that stress us out? For example, we are stressed over other folk's issues instead of our inward longing and desires that will place us in the presence of God. Free yourself from assumptions you have about others that are not full of fruitful possibilities.

Write down some of the assumptions and thoughts you have about others
- Racially
- Religiously
- Politically
- Where are those assumptions rooted and cemented?
- Who planted those seeds?
- How have you made decisions based on faltering conclusions?

Don't be so concerned with Next that you miss Now

If you can't tell, I love basketball. Once I sat behind the bench at a basketball game for a local college. The team they were playing just went on a long run of three straight scores. Anyone who has been around basketball knows that's the moment to call a timeout. As the players came over to the bench one of the younger benchwarmers kept saying their slogan for the year, "Next Play, Next Play, Next Play." An older player grabbed his jersey in frustration and said, "We need to score now!" That image stuck with me for a while, because he made me think of the countless times I have been consumed with "Next year" that I did not work in my "Now year." Even Jesus tells us that tomorrow has its worries and worship today (Matt. 6:34).

Take a look at your life. What are the items you are so concerned about tomorrow that you have not set a sustainability foundation? If your feet are in one place your eyes must be also. There is no need to be consumed with the next that you are not concerned with the now. My friend Jonah was so concerned with preaching in Nineveh that he missed God speaking to him, calling him and the resources he had. He was so consumed with his assumptions reigning true in Nineveh (next) that he missed the authority and uniqueness he had where he was (now).

This happens all of the time, where we sit in one meeting preparing for the next meeting or using our current job's wi-fi to apply for another job. You can miss the beauty of now when you are too consumed with the next. If you were to receive the "Next" you are dreaming about, have you created a sustainability model that would yield success there? Create depth in your "Now" for "Next" to matter. Focus, build and live into the "Now."

Do not get so caught up in telling yourself you are headed in the right direction that you stop moving in the right direction.

Consistently in my journey as a pastor, I would tell my team that, "We are headed in the right direction." These statements would come after business meetings or contentious worship services. I kept saying the same information repeatedly, hoping that everything would change by the end of the report. As I continued to grow, I realized that reminding myself that we were headed in the right direction was me vocalizing that something in my organization was not headed in the right direction. When I began to name what was in the wrong direction, I ensured we were back in the right direction.

Jonah buys his ticket and heads to Tarshish. On the way to Tarshish, I imagine Jonah had several thoughts in his mind:

- *"Maybe God got it wrong."*
- *"God should be happy I even went to Joppa."*
- *"I've been faithful all my life. I have not had my mantle taken."*
-

If you can remind yourself and expend the energy to tell yourself that you are doing the right thing, you have the power and wherewithal to do the right thing. Reclaim your time by doing what you hope to do and completing what you are hoping to achieve. What is keeping you from being what you keep trying to justify? If you have to remind yourself that you are, what is keeping you from becoming? Jonah's story challenges us never to lose focus on who we are becoming as we become that person.

ENDING THOUGHTS:

Have you given yourself a chance to live?
What are the things that block you from seeing Jesus Clearly in your life?
What words do you use to describe who you are?
How do you talk to yourself?
What and who are the determining factors on your value?

CHAPTER THREE
You Matter Enough to End "That"

_____

Once upon a story, a renowned violinist had the pleasure of playing on the world's most expensive violins. Just before his performance, he shared this piece of information with the attendees. His first selection was beautifully and flawlessly played on the world's most expensive violin. The audience erupted with applause. Then the violinist bowed and without hesitation... Smashed the violin over his knee. The gasp of the audience broke the silence in the concert hall. The violinist gracefully said, "Do not worry, this was only a cheap counterfeit." Then, proceeded to play using the real deal, the world's most expensive violin. Once again, the melodies captivated the audience. Most people could not tell the difference in sound because the instrument's quality was secondary to the performer's skill. You are the instrument. You are a uniquely designed instrument by God. You need to see yourself within that value. Prize yourself. Stop tearing yourself down. Build on your strengths. Don't dwell on your weaknesses. Act and think in ways that make you like you. Celebrate who you are and be the best you can be.

Every Sunday, I end our church worship service by saying the following statement:

"If no one tells you, you are loved, and you are Somebody.
You are the Somebody God Loves.
The Somebody God needs.
The Somebody the world doesn't know they can't live without."

These small affirmations to me are significant. There is the power behind knowing and owning your value. You matter enough to matter. You are important! You are so vital that you have a purpose and can walk in that purpose within the protection of God. He will help you take control of your own life while he is *still* in control.

As you may remember, I had time, quietness, and understanding of my unique design and value in the mountains. I had to outline everything about me. I had to outline my life without hating my life. I had to remain true to myself and face everything within me, the good but mostly the ugly. I knew I could not leave the mountains the same. I concluded that I mattered, I had value, and that my purpose could not move forward with negative thinking.

Before we venture into my thoughts on value, consider this:
- What words do you use to describe who you are?
- How do you talk to yourself?

- What and who are the determining factors on your value?

Get out of Your Feelings

Think about your Monday through Friday. Can you already sense the stress hovering over you? How about this, leave the stress behind. Get out of your feelings. View your week as one full of constant beginnings. New beginnings in your class, in your assigned paper, in your daily readings, podcasts you listen and learn from, in the grind to make money, while raising your children, at the daycare, as you workout to get fit, in your Bible devotions, in the relationships you intentional invest in, engagements with people, watching TV shows, news programs, attending church, participating in church, volunteering in your community, cleaning, putting purpose in your everyday... the list can go on and on. Your life is designed within new beginnings. Regardless of the day of the week, every day, you start somewhere.

And I didn't even mention God!

Life is full of constants here and there, now or later... beginning and endings. We are always pulled in different directions, whether we see it or not. Not to mention the interpersonal interactions we hold with individuals we are not close to. Then mix in our emotions based on the weather or recent exchanges, sickness, insecurities, guilt, and shame. There is a lot of activity in one day; it takes much more than a coffee cup to balance all of our day's demands. We haven't even mentioned our tedious and marvelous to-do lists, important follow-up contacts, and meetings. Talk about chaos! What if I told you that all of that is unnecessary? Let me share a secret with you. God did not design you to live a life of chaos. The world has lured us into believing there is no other way of living but continually being on the go and immersed in busyness. Most of us begin tasks we were never designed to take on. In other words, necessary endings must take place for new beginnings to take place. I refuse to believe that in heaven God will verify my to-do list, inspect what phone calls I made, or double-check if I went "viral." To make necessary endings and start new beginnings, you must get out of your feelings. Remove preconceived notions of God and the authority of others over you. Rest in God, get out of your feelings.

Listen to the wisdom of Christ in Matthew 11:28-30 (the Message), *"Are you tired? Worn out? Burned out on religion? Come to me. Getaway with me and you'll recover your life. I'll show you how to take a real rest. Walk with me and work with me—watch how I do it. Learn the unforced rhythms of grace. I won't lay anything heavy or ill-fitting on you. Keep company with me and you'll learn to live freely and lightly."*

Don't miss out on transformational moments because you are not willing to stop and be transformed.

As we engage in deepening your deep wells and engaging with your core values, own these statements:

- That email can still be sent tomorrow.
- That text can be read tomorrow.
- That television show will not change your life
- That status will be there in 25 minutes.

You are worth the time. The betterment of who you are is essential. God provides transformational opportunities every day, even if that transformation is the *ending* of something. Sounds much like the writer of Ecclesiastes 7:8, which reads, "Better is the ending of a thing than its beginning." You are worth it. Who you have been created to deserve to be sought out. How do you do that? Review your current persona and make necessary endings to everything standing before you and who God has created you to be. You are worth ending the unnecessary from your circle, space, and thinking process! You are worth the deletion of that which does not affirm your identity. You are the only person responsible for bringing to fruition who God created you to be. Your life, your whole being, was carefully designed by God. End what is against your value.

Settling is for Sore Losers

Playing basketball is one of my favorite pastimes. Late in a game in high school, my coach always used to tell us, "Never settle for a bad shot." As arrogant high schoolers, we shot when we wanted and did what we wanted. We held little value for the "play." It was not until I worked with video and statistics in college that I learned about settling for bad shots. There are high percentage shots in basketball, shots that are anywhere in the court's painted area. The worst shots to take are the "Long 2's" or any shot inside the 3-point line and not in the paint. In other words, settling for a bad shot. Statistically, the most talented shooters in any professional league still make a low percentage of bad shots. Why? Because if you settle, you are lowering your opportunity for success.

There is no settling in the kingdom of God. God never calls us to settle. God calls us to build, uproot, plant, move, add, grow, go to a new city, and dust your feet off (Jeremiah 1:10). Settling for anything below God's standards is not an option. Settling is for sore losers. You are a winner with God. God never made it okay to settle. He created you to take hold of heaven's opportunity. Settling is not a people issue, it is you and God issue. The moment you get comfortable at a place you need to move from, you have settled in your time with God. There is more with God, don't settle for safe. Instead, work harder for what God grants with grace. But don't confuse busyness and frustration with success. Keep your focus on God, let him lead you into your true self. If you practice what God instructs and work within the challenges he sets forth, I guarantee that the success you are looking for will come. Consider what is on your shoulders that you do not need to carry. Choose to care about you as much as the people who don't like you care about you.

Use the energy you have to rest in your ability.

Change begins with a decision. What you think about is what you will bring about. Change begins and ends with you because hidden in our habits' routine is a prophecy of where we are going. The places you are most passionate about can go two ways. They become places of freedom because of sacrifice or bondage because of a lack of sacrifice. I want to challenge you to change your mind about your freedom. Pursue the opportunity to rest in your passions instead of running to make life happen.

Consider your time. When you think about where you spend most of your time, are those places a space of idolatry? Are you sacrificing at the feet of the leaders around you? Is your sacrifice to the God of the minimum wage, to the God of a paycheck? It is easy to live in fear of getting sick because you are worried about what coworkers may say. Refuse to live in fear of walking on the fragility of someone else's insecurity, by changing your voice or vision to make someone else comfortable. Trust me, with a toddler in our home, I have walked on eggshells. Eggshells are not pleasant. Therefore, I prefer to sweep away the trash that slows down my progress. My energy is set on resting in my ability, and so should yours.

By no means am I telling you to drop out of school, quit your job, and run into the forest like John the Baptist (Matthew 3:1). If you have begun to worship your workplace, you need to kill that idol. Where you spend most of your time, even if it's in the church, should not be worshipped. The church is a place to practice worship! God says to the people of Israel in Amos 5:5, "Seek me and live! Avoid the destruction that God will heap on idol worshippers and the idols themselves. Think of where you are investing your time and thoughts. If it is not God, begin to make changes.

What if the energy you have used to run away from God at work, you used to rest with God at work? Be very bold with your boundaries. Your time in any space can be fruitful if the seeds you sow are falling on fertile ground. Bold boundaries create creativity. Demand the respect you deserve because God respects you. Demand the Honor you deserve because God honors you. Engage in only what God calls you to do, be relentless with your "No."
Rest is not a luxury, it's a necessity.

Ready for another Basketball analogy? I was coaching a third-grade girls' team once and it was so much fun to see these young ladies grow. One day in practice I taught them how to sweep the ball away from their defender. Sweeping the ball meant bending your knees, bringing the ball to the highest point on one side, and violently, rapidly moving the ball to the other side to create separation from the defender. Simple enough right? One of the players decided this was her favorite move. She grabbed the ball and all she did was keep sweeping. She did not stop sweeping the ball. To the point where one of her teammates had to come and steal the ball from her because she was stopping anyone else from practicing.

Many times, we develop tunnel vision on things that truly do not matter. We miss out on what God is trying to show us and become exhausted going through the motions. Rest is essential for our focus, we must keep it a priority and hold ourselves accountable. Without rest, we begin to resent. After all, tired people become tempted people. Sweeping through emails, staff meetings, classes and work becomes second nature, we lose focus on what truly matters. When that sweeping mentality carries itself into the home, that's when danger awaits. We then begin to sweep rest. We prioritize watching television instead of meaningful conversations with our family. We forget to check-in on our spouse, we lose desire to know how their day has been. We lose. We become lost in sweeping left and right, rather than taking a pause, resting, and focusing on the true priority. Woe to us when your child becomes your alarm clock and you resent them. Make rest a priority.

What doesn't make your calendar? Think about it... It's intentional time with God and our loved one. Put God on your calendar. Put your Family on your Calendar. Relentlessly work to keep them on.

ENDING THOUGHTS:

o   What meetings do you *not* need to have?
o   What in person meetings need to be on the phone?
o   What opportunities do you *not* need to take advantage of?
o   What coworkers/classmates do you just need to let go of?
o   What and who do you need to release energy from?

CHAPTER FOUR
Ending to Feeling Sorry for myself

Welcome! You have finally made it to the necessary endings portion!

The first funeral I had in Vermont's mountains was over every word and thought that made me feel sorry for who I was. Thoughts ranged from personal anecdotes, to shorthand sketches, and simple words. It was a painful moment but critical moment. My thoughts and self-talk were detrimental to who I was. Negative self-talk marred the divine artistry that was at work within me. It was ridden with comparison and insecurity.

In many cases, unchecked insecurities lead to pride-filled actions, which was my case. The entirety of this chapter confronts some of the language we use against ourselves to hopefully lead you to have a mindset that, *"Casts down imagination, and every high thing that comes against the knowledge of God, and bring into captivity every thought to the obedience of Christ"* (2 Corinthians 10:5). Change is possible. Your thoughts and self-talk changes you and those around you. Stop feeling sorry for yourself and begin to live the life you were designed to live.

Hot weight is easy weight

My son is full of so much life. One of our Saturday traditions is laundry. The last load is always comforters and towels. We always wait until the comforters are at its hottest temperature in the drying machine, remove the scorching hot comforter from the machine and run to throw it on anyone in sight! It's a lot of fun for us. While this imagery seems childish, that's the imagery we get in scripture regarding how the divine sees our anxiety and how we handle it. In 1 Peter 5:7, the writer tells us to take the anxiety, the hottest cover we have and throw it on God. Beautiful right? But guess what? Some things are cute in concept until a commitment is required. 1 Peter 5:7 challenges us to see the power of God and the weakness of our mind games. Our shoulders were never equipped with the ability to handle anxiety. They are equipped to set ourselves free. Life brings all of us into new challenges and seasons. No matter how positive or negative the space you are in is, a new season brings about new worries, problems, and opportunities.

Being committed to not feeling sorry for yourself is honoring a commitment to see yourself how God sees you. Maybe one of the reasons you picked this book up is because you are wrestling with the constant anxiety of your self-value and worth. Your mental well-being is unhealthy and your self-talk has become self-hatred. A challenge to view yourself the way that God views you is a clarion call beyond the mental jails we have not only admitted ourselves to, but our insecurities keep us in.

Think about it. You start going to a new gym and the same people you used to pace yourself are no longer there. While you are working out, it's different to pace yourself with new faces and music. You are losing weight but mentally it's not the same. Imagine you lose an enemy to death. The individual you were competing against is no longer there for you to wrestle with. Every new season opens new opportunities. Do not overlook the wisdom you can develop because you are unwilling to confront your weaknesses.

Success comes to those who are actively pouring into their deep wells. Wells that keep you humble and hungry because you are pouring and pulling from your uniqueness. Humility becomes the ground where success is birthed. Anxiety enters when the success we hope for does not spring as fast or strong as we desire.

Consider this:
- What are some of your weaknesses?
- What makes you anxious?
- What are you constantly apologizing for?

What is Anxiety?
In a contentious time at my first church, we had three business meetings a year. Personally, I knew of a couple attendees who despised these meetings. Nevertheless, these meetings were needed. The hate for these meetings became so strong that it became very personal. My wife and son began getting stalked to the point where someone tried picking up my son up from daycare, without my consent or my wife's. I tried to be civil, but that had been the last straw. When the meeting day came, I entered the room with fists

raised. I was angry, frustrated, and ready to fight anyone who came in my path. All of a sudden, my watch began to violently vibrate. The screen on my watch pulled up the emergency number to dial. I was confused, but quickly caught on that my heart rate had escalated so fast that my watch thought I was having a heart attack. Only it was not a heart attack, it was a panic attack. I remember the stiffness of my body, I was frozen. My body would not move. I could not think clearly. When I finally summoned the strength, I walked out of the room and began to breathe. I had created so many narratives of how that meeting would go and what those intentionally trying to hurt my family would say, that I had let them lead me into heart attack symptoms. Nothing actually happened, but I willed my body to suggest that something might happen.

Anxiety turns rational fear into a runaway train of emotions. Soon, "What if something happens" becomes "When something happens." Anxiety causes us to hyper-focus on what could be, leading to an overwhelming sense of worry, nervousness, and unease. It cripples us socially and costs us relationally. But life does not have to be this way. I have struggled with anxiety, panic attacks and situational depression off and on for years. Sometimes it grows with persistent problems in my life. Other times it comes on with no apparent reason. I've even asked God why He doesn't just take my life. However, as 2 Corinthians 5:14 says, "Christ's love compels us." God has always brought me up from my lowest points; His love truly never fails (Ps. 100:5).

God is challenging all of us to come out of our feelings and walk into our future. Anxiety exists when the problems around you overwhelm the peace within you. Stop trying to hide your anxiety. It's okay to not be okay. We cannot resolve that anxiety is a part of life. There is something much better for you than to live with constant anxiety. If your solution to anxiety isn't with Jesus and the peace he offers, you are fighting a forest fire with a squirt gun. God can quiet your anxious mind.

Anxiety will position us where things that do not make sense start to make sense. Things that are contrary to your future have a larger domain than your future. Anxiety will position you were little things that don't matter start to matter. Anxiety will remind you about your insecurities.

Think of the places you get anxious; these are the areas in which you attempt to disqualify yourself from where God has qualified you. For example:

- Your Marriage
- Parenthood
- Why was I selected to be healed?
- Why am I the one called
- Why am I blessed in my 80s?
- Why is the job calling me back?

When I am anxious, I am telling myself, I am less than. That I am not able, all because I am insecure about my gift. How can we proclaim that we are changing communities when we allow anxiety to keep us from community? Paul even recognized this tendency and told the Galatians,

"Make a careful exploration of who you are and the work you have been given, and then sink yourself into that. Don't be impressed with yourself. Don't compare yourself with others. Each of you must take responsibility for doing the creative best you can with your own life" (Galatians 6:4-5 MSG).

What if what God is calling you to do is demanding you to deepen your courage? Anxiety can and will undo your marriage, career, faith, and happiness. It tells you the lie that what you have isn't enough and you can't own the joy of the loss. We start clamoring for more, thinking that the "Next" is what we need. You can miss the blessings of God around you because you are so concerned with what you lack. I used to lie to myself and say, "Everything is fine," or, "I'm okay" when secretly I was battling anxiety and discontentment. The number of pills, home remedies, and doctors' appointments I had for falsified realities would amaze you. The first funeral held at a mountain in Vermont was a face to face confrontation to my discontentment. I was determined to hold on to my joy and gain perspective. A fixed perspective allowed me to concentrate on what God has done and is doing, rather than thinking about what I don't have.

Necessary endings are revealed when you ask Jesus the right questions, Jesus will give you the answer you need. It is not a challenge of doing more, it is a challenge of a greater God-driven awareness. Church calls it discernment. Think about it, we live by being told what matters instead of discerning what matters. You don't want what's next if you are comfortable with the unnecessary attachments that are killing your spirit. If it does not enhance or promote your well-being, it needs to be destroyed! Anxiety can cause us to miss Jesus standing in front of us because we are anxious about what life will be without him. The good news is you can break through anxiety with a thankful heart.

I'm not saying that we should do nothing about anxiety or depression. When the nature of Christ's love compels me beyond myself, then there must be action! So, what can we do amid anxiety or depression right now? Christ's love compels us to get up and keep on living. Christ's love compels us to look in the mirror and see a valuable person, a person for whom Christ died! The process of healing is never a waste. Our anxiety or depression might be used one day to encourage someone else. Both the journey and the necessary ending becomes our testimony.

Don't address with your flesh what you can attack with your faith

I love old TV shows. One of those shows was *Different Strokes*. It's funny. If you have never watched it, it was about Arnold and Willis. They lived in the projects but with time made their way to living in a penthouse. The whole show revolved around Arnold and Willis getting used to living in the penthouse while maintaining some project tendencies. Old patterns are challenging to shy away from, especially when they become part of our identity. When God found you and me, we were in the spiritual projects. When we converted to walk with him, he brought us to a place where we were

44

qualified. Are you willing to leave some project mentalities behind to live in the world God had brought you to? What in your mind causes you to be distant from the Father? What in your life do you to disqualify yourself, when the Lord has set otherwise? Attack that! It is an official "Time Out" for the authority we have given to our self-made foolishness. We have allowed access to our emotional wellness's intricacies to be disturbed by people who are not invested in our best! Today, we say "Time Out." I challenge you to fight for your new life. I challenge you to attack what makes you care so much about others that you have forgotten your possibility. Do not be an enemy to your potential. The skin you have been given is anointed to disturb glass ceilings. Recognize yourself by working on yourself.

It is "Time Out" for only addressing situations that our destruction can yield more extensive results. You have not been selected to address it. You have been chosen to attack it. Do not be lazy in your call and don't settle for the least. Creation is waiting for you to create. Attack what is against your future with the stronger faith than the broadest view of your imagination. Attack faithfully what your flesh is tepid to address.

Quit asking for more strength and Ask God to reveal his Strength

Go into any bookstore or search online and you will find that the top books sold are self-help books. In those works, are chapters full of comparison and competition. After the author admonishes the reader, they can become the greatest by achieving more and stepping on others. How?

- Lead through manipulative language.
- Eat by altering your diet to the model of a celebrity who can afford a full-time trainer.
- Change by becoming someone inauthentic but call it authentic.

It is no wonder the rise of millennials and generation-z living with functional depression. That is, self-hatred that can make enough money to continue the self-hatred. It's okay if I give you another Bible story, right?

Doubting Thomas is my homeboy. I think he gets a terrible reputation. Jesus and the disciples have been kicking it for almost three years. They had been taught and engaged by Jesus before he was killed by the state. In the middle of Passover, a massive celebration for the Jews, Jesus pulls all of the disciples into an upper room for dinner. After Jesus washes their feet Jesus tells them he is going to the Father and challenges the disciples to love each other because it is by their dedication that the community will know they are disciples.

Jesus gives another speech in John 14:1-5 where he tells the Disciples, "In my father's house are many mansions, if there weren't, I would have told you. I am going away to prepare a place for you. I will come back and get you so you will be with me. You know the way I am going." It's beautiful, right? Look at Thomas' response...

"What Way?"

Well here's the full scripture:
"Do not let your hearts be troubled. You believe in God [a]; believe also in me. My Father's house has many rooms; if that were not so, would I have told you that I am going there to prepare a place for you? And if I go and prepare a place for you, I will come back and take you to be with me that you also may be where I am. You know the way to the place where I am going." Thomas said to him, "Lord, we don't know where you are going, so how can we know the way?" (John 14:1-5).

"What Way"

Before we jump on Thomas, this is a statement many of us have asked Jesus. We get comfortable knowing Jesus will until we are reminded that God will use us to show that he can. This type of skepticism and question from Thomas is pervasive throughout scripture. The early church expected for the fullness of God to manifest on the earth, to a point that Stephen states later that he would wait for it (Acts 6:8-15). For Jesus to tell them that he is leaving is a big shock to the mind and spirit. Thomas did not respond with doubt, he responded with his love for Jesus! He screams, "What Way!" I want to be a part of the movement of Jesus, What Way? Where are you needing clarity from God on your future? What Way!

Be grown and unafraid enough to have honest and full conversations with God. Not questioning God but willing to ask God questions. Wrestle with the difficult questions of life. Be someone who will not stop at a one hour of study or service or be comfortable with the easy answer. Still, people like Thomas will sit at the table

47

with Jesus and risk their reputation and perception. Why? Because you love Jesus so much that you are willing to be the revelation of God's power in the world!

God trusts you so much that He will use you to be the picture of his authority. It is okay to not be the strong one all of the time. As a pastor, my most challenging conversations are not before funerals, but after funerals. When someone passes there is always one relative that is strong for everyone else who visits. That healthy person needs space and a shoulder the same way we need one. It is okay not to always be strong and allow God to be the strong one. What would your life look like if you stopped asking God to give you more strength and asked him to show you how strong God is?

Get your weight up.

Glory is used in the Greek is the word *doxa,* where we get the word doxology from. It is another word for the word weight. This same word is what we see in a description of how planets are pulled in order. The sun's gravitational weight keeps our planets stable orbit and the right distances from each other. The same can be applied to the glory of God. God's weight in your life can pull things into order. It will allow you to have a posture of gratitude to extinguish anxiety. It will enable you to have clarity on the Nature of God while bearing witness to the activity of God. It will force you to be in awe of God while simultaneously pulling you closer to God and the infinite possibilities inside of you. God can and will pull things in order.

Recognize where you have gone off track. No insecurity about you cannot be conquered. Never settle for what anxiety pulls out of you, you are not called to settle. You are called to the season to soar. Ask our divine God to pull you in order, to grab ahold of anything out of order and keep you straight on the possibility within you. Why? Your anxiety doesn't have to kill you, it can accelerate you. Give God full control.

I want to end this chapter by giving you three concrete steps of acceleration. I love cooking and I have learned that little salt can go a long way:

Laugh a little- For you straight faced, sourpuss, solemn folk who believe you have nothing to laugh at, read this next sentence carefully. Take all of your clothes off, that's right, strip naked. Now stand in front of a mirror and sing to yourself. If that doesn't make you laugh grab your old high school yearbook and check out the style you thought was so hip! Find space to laugh more. Even stressful experiences produce laughter material. Use some post-it notes to write down what makes you laugh or brings humor to your life. Keep those with you. My family has a practice where we dance for 5 minutes every single day. The therapeutic nature of accountable dancing in our home has yielded much fruit in laughter. Laughter is cheap but good medicine. It distracts your attention, changes your attitude, and causes relaxation.

Live a little- An author I love called, "Anonymous" once said, "The problem with life is that it's so daily." Life compels us to make the most of our daily existence and possibilities, along with the challenges and setbacks. While we may be living longer, are we living well? Live my friends! I am a strong proponent of nature and travel. By no means is living regulated to those two experiences only. Rather I challenge you to go to someplace where you can see God's glory manifest. Where you can create an experience that centers you and you can find yourself in the world.

Learn a little- You are at the end of a chapter of a book! You are almost to the end. Keep reading and learning. Hal Stebbins said, "Perpetual hunger is the key to a full mind. When you stop learning you stop." Soak up as much knowledge as you can so your knowledge can create spaces for you to pour that knowledge into the world. Get informed and stay informed. Such thinking will produce knowledge that when applied will have substantial payoff.

This was my first funeral. It was not easy. I wrote things down that I hated and disliked about myself and watched them turn into ashes. Little did I know that-that freedom would open the door for more profound clarity in what comes next. Let's keep burning!

ENDING THOUGHTS:

o   What are some of your weaknesses?
o   What makes you anxious?
o   What are you constantly apologizing for?

SCRIPTURES

2 Corinthians 10:5 | 1 Peter 5:7 | 2 Corinthians 5:14 | Galatians 6:4-5

CHAPTER FIVE
Ending Caring About "They"

_____

I went back into my tiny home and grabbed the next set of notes. I was free, or so I thought. I saw how many of the notes had someone else's name on it. A lot of my self hatred was in the hands of people who did not know they had control over my decision making and lifestyle choices. I had given so many people power that were unaware they had such authority. I had considered people enemies that did not know they were enemies, to a point where I even hated some of the people I was called to pastor. It is hard to pray for people you cannot stand. It is hard to pray for people who you are worshipping. This world has done a disservice to many of us by basing success in others' hands, namely their words over us and the assumptions we have about them. (Cancel Culture anyone?) I knew for me this was the obvious next step, to burn the association I had with the various people and have a necessary ending to caring about the "They" in my life. I loved cutting people off, until I actually cut people off.

High School Muses

I don't know what type of High School you went to but let

me tell you about mine. The cool kids, the weird kids, the smart kids, the athletic kids, and the "other" kids. No one knew how to define the "other" type of kids, "they" were just different. Maybe they were doing video work, listening to different music types, or dressing out of what we considered normal. No one knows why we ostracized them. It was High School.

Looking back, we ostracized those who were unafraid to accomplish the things we wish we could. Our labels kept them at arm's length, our own insecurities fed off of their strength. One we wished we had. I want to challenge you to consider the grouping of people around you. Who are the people you look at differently because their skillset/talent is different than yours? What would you be able to accomplish if you destroyed the comparison trap? What if you used your abilities to build a world with them rather than around them?

"They-ing" or "Them-ing" if you will is an interesting concept. It is beyond otherizing, or another-izing. While other-izing speaks to ostracization, them-ing speaks to unnecessary labels. Labels that separate people who are not the other, but our jealousy forbids us for being jealous of our future. Have you ever noticed how innately we find ways to separate ourselves from others calling it "Inclusion?" Think about it. If "Black Lives Matter" then other lives do not. If "Blue Lives Matter," then other experiences do not. In the name of "Community," we separate. We care so much about what title someone else gives us instead of the title you own and create. The constant concern about the label's others have showered on you to limit you, distracts you from the limitless nature of your possibility.

One day, I traveled through South Dakota through Black Hills near Mount Rushmore and ran into a snowstorm losing all types of direction. There was a white out storm and I needed to make it to my hotel. Luckily, I found a snowplow that was clearing a road and began to follow it. After a while, the plow driver got out of the truck and walked to my car. "Sir, where are you headed?" he asked. I responded, the name of my hotel. He answered, "Well you need to leave this parking lot. I am plowing a parking lot not a street." I never felt more foolish! Not getting anywhere fast forces us to decide exactly where we wish to go and to achieve. Blindly succumbing to others' opinions and deciding to follow their paths may lead you to mindlessly wander through a parking lot when you could be reaching safety.

Every person reading this book is different. I know that. Move from learning to owning. When you own your differences, you create space to make a mark with your differences. God is not surprised you are different, God designed you that way. What keeps us from owning and living into our differences as a means of self-liberation instead of community isolation is caring too much about "They."

Oh, you know "They"
- "They" don't like me.
- "They" hate me.
- "They" always talk about me.
- "They" (insert your statement here)

Whomever "They" are I want to challenge you to destroy the thinking pattern built on "They." As quiet as it is kept, "They" do not care, you just really want them to care as much as you do not care about your future.

This is the ending of caring:
- What "They" think.
- What "They" do.
- What 'They" say.

For a year at my church, I committed to not talk about the "Haters" and "Enemies." Here's why. As a part of my dissertation, I researched manuscripts and sermonic expressions from White, Black, and LatinX pastors. The Pastors I compared, were all men and women who:

- Attended Liberal Arts Universities.
- Earned a Masters or Doctorate level degree.
- Took similar scriptures about Love in one of the four synoptic Gospels.
- All exegetical and expositional preachers.

Here's what I learned:

There was a stark difference in black/brown and white preachers. Beyond the sheer expression of Blackness and

Brownness, white preachers preached contextual sermons that built community with those who are my neighbor and those who I think are my neighbor. White preachers, acknowledged that the only enemy is the evil one (Satan). If anyone is infested with demonic forces you speak to the devil because all of us through prayer and fasting have the authority to cast out demons. When communicating about the community they never get caught up because God calls us to live in a community.

When it came to my friends from the diaspora, Black preachers, here is what we talked about. Every sermon said the same word at least once, "Haters." How to handle them, how to destroy them, how to get rid of them, you get the picture. They were great sermons that kept our focus on the text's people, not Jesus unless we embodied him. While I loved the sermons, it showed something I did not expect. In black preaching traditions, we do a great job demonizing and/or deifying people. This is not liberation work, it is community destroying work. The same "Hater" that we are destroying at one church is at another church thinking about destroying you. It is no wonder income levels and disparity exist among low-middle class black and brown bodies! These sermons did not dedicate space to grow beyond good into extraordinary. They were perfect, everyone else is terrible, and I made it to church I am the hated. Unsustainable church killing self-help foolishness. We cannot keep baptizing our foolishness!

"They"

I am tired of how easy it has become to demonize people, we have spent so much time hating people and causing hatred of other people. By no means am I telling you to be best friends with everyone. I want to wake up a mindset. We have gotten comfortable spending so much time hating other people that God has positioned in our space to help awaken dreams for the future. We have spent too much time talking and thinking about people that we dismiss ourselves, or the idea that our success can only come at the expense of someone else's demise. (Side note, we never talk about when we are the "Hater!")

This "Them-ing," "They-ing," hateration, cancel culture, creates a language that says "They" do not deserve life, a job, life, children, a future. It sounds like this is our prayer, "God I know you're God but God you got it wrong with that person. So, if you would excuse yourself off your throne, make sure they are hurt, down, depressed. Because there is a part of me that I have not given over to you to deal with my hatred towards one of your gifts to the world. I want to take control of how you treat them because they do not deserve life. In Jesus Name. Amen."

Too often in our spaces, we have done a great job demonizing others, deifying ourselves and then saying God fix it on the other side.

So, here's the necessary ending. End Caring About "They"

- What "They" think.
- What "They" do.
- What 'They" say.

Consider this. Think about your past 12 months:

- How much time have you given to thinking about "They?"
- How much energy did you give to "They?"
- Think about the food you haven't eaten, counseling sessions you have had, nights you have not slept and anger you had all over them.
- How many phone conversations have you had this year talking about "They" when you could have been praying about how to lead them to Christ.

Who are they?

- They – Coworker
- They – Family member
- They – Church member
- They – Classmate

Ending Caring About What They Think.

Why? Because, "They" are not worth the energy you can give to the divine, your work ethic, your future, and your dreams! Free yourself from caring about them. Why? Because if "They" can strip this from you that means they don't care about you. If you can think that someone negatively about you, there is no positivity coming from those foolish discussions and thoughts.

How do we move past this? How can you heal this? Know this. The "They" you cannot stand are full of infinite possibilities and a great opportunity. They have a story, and you have a story.

They have a future, and you have a future. There is something about your worst "Enemy" that Jesus died for. Jesus did not give you the authority to figure out why he died for them. Jesus wants your attention to live into the reasons He died for you. If you are so consumed with why Jesus lives for them, you forget caring why Jesus died for you.

It does not matter!

This is not an easy practice. Many of the relationships we consider "They" relationships are consumed by people who we once had fruitful relationships with, that fizzled or were fractured. The issue was an unfulfilled expectation. Mismanaged interpersonal conflict can destroy the best of any relationship no matter the character of the people involved. Often the problem communicated is not the issue that traumatized. Get to the core, the root issue and take that to God. Here is what I learned at this funeral.

Forgive yourself for bowing at the altar of someone else's forgiveness or affirmation

When I first started preaching, I was blessed to preach at a large church in my hometown. When I finished preaching the worst sermon I have ever preached an older woman came up to me and said, "Baby, that was great!" At that moment everything flipped for me. That was the best sermon I had ever preached! My language changed because one person affirmed me. It made me ask myself, what if I lived into the affirmation of the divine more than I sought affirming the people around me. At that moment, her voice mattered more than the voice that imparted the word into me. Beyond God's voice, too often we give that same energy to the people whose malicious intent is to keep you distracted from your future. Woven throughout biblical text are people who did many things God hated, they created idols. Those idols distracted and took away from the time they had to worship the true and living God. In negative relationships, we are so indebted to "They" talk because we are frozen in awe of the power we have told them they have over us. Therefore, you cannot move forward without their affirmation or forgiveness. Think of the negative emails, statuses, and phone calls you have had in hopes that "They" heard you were talking about them so you can give them a "Piece of your mind." As humorous as that thought is, it is a serious thing! You're not presenting your best, you are offering what others want. Free yourself from affirmation. Yes, life does position us in need of a pat on the back. Don't idolize the pat!

As a kid the Univer-soul circus came to town. It was an all-black circus replete with all of the normal circus acts in our community. Crowds of people came to see the circus. I was so enamored with the elephants. We attended a production on the main stage. I noticed how one of the elephants was content being held down by a simple wooden stake in the ground. I asked my mother, "Why doesn't the elephant just get up and pull the wood out of the ground and run away? He's big enough!" My mom laughed and said, "They've trained him to think the wood is stronger than it really is."

As I grew up I learned that circuses train small elephants as babies to be connected to steel stakes in cement that they cannot move. As they get older they are accustomed to not controlling their movements so wooden stakes are equated to steel stakes. While they can pull it out of the ground, they have given the stake too much power. Have you been so conditioned in relationships that they keep you hostage? What your parents thought or that one situation in work became a stake that keeps you seeking affirmation and limited. Run away my friends! Creation is waiting.

Forgiveness does not mean reconciliation

Everything that is broken does not need to come back together. I have often heard that if someone wrongs you forgive them, and then reconcile. Reconciliation speaks to the reuniting of the relationship regardless of the brokenness. If the relationship was fractured and does not yield fruit for the destiny you live into, forgive yourself for bringing back together what needs to stay apart. Reconciliation asks the question: Does this relationship at her best build the kingdom of God? If not… Forgive and keep it moving. You do not need to be friends. Some relationships are not welcome in the places where you are headed and where you are praying for. Life is too beautiful to be marred by dysfunctional relationships.

Forgiveness is like looking at an old cut on your body that has become a scar. When the cut was fresh it was painful. Over time, it is only a visible scar of forgotten pain. It is possible to get beyond the pain of a relationship, but the scar will always tell the story. Are you willing to have a relationship with your scar? Do not live in resentment because resentment causes us to re-feel our wounds, while forgiveness heals the wounds. Healing does not mean you re-position yourself to be wounded again. As we pray for relationships that build the kingdom of God some need to stay apart to effectively build the kingdom of God. Forgive yourself for the need to be friends with everyone. There will be people who cannot stand you, dislike your future, cause chaos, and distract you from what you know is inside of you. Do not deny your future because you are trying to remake one good day from the past.

Winning people is better than winning arguments

My son has a piggy bank in his room. As my wife and I were attempting to potty train him, we incentivized him by telling him he would get one of his favorite toys with the piggy bank's money. Everytime he used the potty, money would go into the piggy bank. As he used the potty, the amount of money in the bank increased and his excitement to purchase a toy grew. Visualize your energy as a currency. Consider this, winning people to work for a more significant cause than you is the gift from your energy (Read that again). Your breath is too expensive to be wasted on an argument or unnecessary worry that is not worth your time. An old African proverb says, "When two elephants fight, the only thing that suffers is the grass." There are always unintended consequences felt by the weak in unnecessary conflict. Whenever we live into winning an argument, we say that our pride is more important than the community built with our words. Your words have the ability to build instead of destroy. Win people more than seeking to win an argument!

Let me give you some scripture. If I will challenge you to end caring what people think, how do we practically do this? Paul wrote a short letter to one of his favorite little churches, the church at Philippi. As he wrote his crescendo, if you will, he said, "I press on towards the mark for the prize of the higher calling" (Phil.3:14). In Lester terms, I want the prize Jesus has for me in heaven because there is nothing on earth that people can give me that will give me the type of gift that Jesus can give. This gift is explained in Chapter 4.

"Rejoice in the Lord always. I will say it again: Rejoice! Let your gentleness be evident to all. The Lord is near. Do not be anxious about anything, but in every situation, by prayer and petition, with thanksgiving, present your requests to God. And the peace of God, which transcends all understanding, will guard your hearts and your minds in Christ Jesus. Finally, brothers and sisters, whatever is true, whatever is noble, whatever is right, whatever is pure, whatever is lovely, whatever is admirable—if anything is excellent or praiseworthy—think about such things. Whatever you have learned or received or heard from me, or seen in me—put it into practice. And the God of peace will be with you" (Phil. 4:4-7).

Consider the Message translation:
"Summing it all up, friends, I'd say you'll do best by filling your minds and meditating on things true, noble, reputable, authentic, compelling, gracious—the best, not the worst; the beautiful, not the ugly; things to praise, not things to curse. Put into practice what you learned from me, what you heard and saw and realized. Do that, and God, who makes everything work together, will work you into his most excellent harmonies" (Phil. 4:8-9 MSG).

Paul is communicating what it means to build a community. He tells the church to stand firm in their hope because that hope is what will keep you upright when life wants to knock you down, therefore, Rejoice! In this constant rejoicing, Paul gives a list of things that can grant peace that transcends understanding and guards your heart. This is the key to losing care about "They." He tells them, and you, to discern:

- What is true
- What is noble
- What is right
- What is pure
- What is lovely
- What is admirable

There's your litmus test.
- Each of those words means something different.
- What is true: What cannot be disproven. For his community, that which comes directly from Christ.
- What is noble: What yields self-respect. Literally, what does not strip you of Honor, but brings you Honor.
- What is right: The broadest of all of the words. The best way to understand this is righteous when it comes to your discernment and wisdom.
- What is pure: Free from any sort of defilement.
- What is lovely: Whatever would attract the hearts of pure souls.
- What is admirable: Whatever would excite the souls of pure people.

There have been many times that I have preached this particular set of scripture. Each time I have urged individuals to think differently, carefully considering what things fit into our lives that fit into these definitions. When you look at the scope of your life, how would you define the words from Paul?

- What is true for you?
- What is noble for you?
- What is right for you?
- What is pure for you?
- What is lovely for you?
- What is admirable for you?

The answers to these questions should shift your focus to the items in your life that enhance and highlight who you are. Think, is this conversation, relationship, status, engagement, class, time together, the answer to one of my questions? If not, it will not yield peace and most likely open the door for frustration. Take control of your life by negating the things trying to control your life and strip you of the experiences that will give you a chance to sow power into this world. Take control of your focus and that will take care of your actions. Whomever "They" are, is just a distraction. Distractions are nothing more than the inner denial of your future. Refuse to allow anything to strip you of concrete focus. Distractions are not worth your health when you can alter the trajectory of culture.

The Bible admonishes us, "Do not let the sun go down on your wrath" (Eph. 4:26 NKJV). As a sophomore in college my roommate and I disagreed a lot. He was a great person, we were just two 19-year-olds. One day we got into an issue over something trivial. My pride took a beating and made me upset. I was bitter towards every person I encountered even to a point that I gave my roommate the silent treatment when I saw him around campus. I happened to open my Bible and it came to the scripture mentioned above. I said to the Lord, "God, keep the sun up longer." I realized that my feelings were not healthy and I could change my attitude and help the relationship. So, I tell you, tell the sun to go down. Whatever you need to handle before it goes down, handle it. Nothing deserves the attention that needs God to shift heaven and earth for your pride or someone else's pride.

As you read this chapter who are the "They" that kept coming to your mind? Who are the "They" that distracted you from grabbing ahold of the principles that can loosen their grip on your thinking? What if you stopped caring what they think and you reminded yourself of who you are? You are worth it. They do not deserve the power.

ENDING THOUGHTS:

Take a moment and define what is true, noble, right, pure, lovely, and admirable for you. Allow those definitions to give you direction to where the Lord is calling you.

SCRIPTURES

Philippians 3:14 | Philippians 4:4-9 | Ephesians 4:26

CHAPTER SIX
The Ending Of Your Last Dream

_____

I was halfway through these funerals, and I felt so free, I left my tiny home and went through the community in Vermont. It was a relatively well-to-do neighborhood with an old gothic local community church. I have a severe affinity and love for beautiful church architecture. I pulled me "I'm a pastor on a break" card and was able to get into the building. After praying with the church's Pastor, she allowed me to spend some time in their facility. I sat and began to stare at the ceiling and windows. In particular, one set of windows depicted the miracles of Jesus in a way I had never seen created before. I was drawn into who was added to the stories according to the artist. My imagination began to wander until that mindless exploration became life-giving. I wrote down in my journal, "Kill your dream so you can see the way God sees." I jumped up and ran to my car, knowing we had some burning to do.

The difference between dreams and vision is discernment. It is one thing to dream about a job, and it is another to know what God said about that dream. Dreams are beautiful, but discernment clarifies that you are not walking down a path that can destroy you.

Dreams lead you to people, vision leads you to God. Dreams with discernment are the vision. Dreams without discernment is a good story. That's why we often love our last dream. We can hold on to our previous dream because our last dream is the space we dwell in, making us comfortable with the potential's mediocre nature. It was a thought and prediction in your head, hoping for a "Someday."

If your last dream was the totality of God's work in your life, then what do you need God for? God can work beyond the biggest dream you have. Refuse to allow your last dream to become your definition. Consider the way you speak to others and about yourself. Often the way we engage with the Divine is based on God answering your last dream. What if God says deepen your discernment level to make sure your dream is not just a dream but a clear vision. If we genuinely believe that God can do exceedingly and abundantly, that means God can go beyond.

Loose and Lose your Dream

We are called to be people of vision. Dreaming is a lost art. Dreaming and visioning have been lost over time. We have dumbed down our dreams to the visions of other people. It is no wonder that anxiety and stress control our thoughts and relationships because of the comparison trap. In this chapter, I want to challenge you to have the necessary ending to your last dream because who you can become is based on who God has called you to be, not based on what you can do better than someone else. Consider some of your most recent dreams and prayers. Dreams that hold a house, car, or life because you've seen it. Your biggest dream is not someone else's reality. Your "Today" is someone else's "Someday," and your "Someday" is someone else's "Today." Know that neither are your ending! We live in a society where dreams have become nothing more than what you think your talent can do better than someone else's achievements and financial gain and not based on the authority in your authenticity. We are not people who are visioning for the future. We are people who are great at comparing and competing. Competition and Comparison will land you in a large ocean called "Settle."

In that ocean, you find ships called:
- Not graduating
- Not applying
- Not having the relationship.
- Not going for that home
- Not going back
- Not going higher
- Not achieving

These ships in the ocean called "Settle" become the boundaries of your dream instead of your dream dictating your boundless possibilities. Whenever we make a choice to settle, it is asking to maintain instead of excel. A lack of excelling becomes a transactional relationship with the Divine that will not let you go beyond normalcy. In other words, we settle into the mundane, repetitive nature of day to day living that makes anything beyond today seemingly unattainable. This is where frustration and anxiety set in and where the insecurities from your past become your leader.

As you read this chapter, kill that thinking. Kill that dream. Kill the dream defined by boundaries seen on social media, lies told to you by your parents, or definitions given to you by the larger society.

- Kill that boundary
- Kill those words
- Kill the past
- Kill the frustration
- Kill the anger
- Kill the hate.

I want to kill the frustrating nature of a dream forbidding you to move beyond your current situation to the future. I am not telling you to stop dreaming! I am telling you to destroy the last dream that has forbidden you from having a concrete vision. I am challenging you to kill Comparison and envision the possibilities that God still has on your life. What is God trying to teach you that you are not allowing him to because you are waiting for God to answer your last dream?

Crucify your Dream

This was the biggest and most monumental funeral. When I put to death my last big dream, I began to gain the necessary clarity on God's vision for me to live into. For me, this comes out of some personal reflection when I was telling God what I wanted to do instead of trusting in what was and is much bigger than me. I created lists because of the countless books I was reading that told me how to "envision." Instead of praying to the Lord to go beyond, I told God to meet me where I was and do things my way. This was until

I learned that God's vision only works with the gifts God has given rather than with a strategy. Culture eats strategy for breakfast, Christ desires my prayer life. God had to crucify the dream.

My journal was explicit this day in the mountains, and I wrote down what the spirit was speaking to me. The Lord said, "How dare you think you are more powerful than Me (God)" "How dare you put Me (God) down at the level of your talent?" "How dare you put Me (God) down to the level of your ability?" "How prideful are you when you placed Me (God) in the boxes of your insecurity and dreamscapes?"

God was frustrated with me. While I don't know you, let me rephrase it to apply to us all.

- How dare you think you are more powerful than God.
- How dare you put down God at the level of your talent?
- How dare you put Go down to the level of your ability?
- Do you know how prideful you are when placing God in the boxes of your insecurity and dreamscapes?"

Aim Higher

During my senior year of college, one of my professors gave us a unique test. She divided the test into three categories, and we were told to pick from one of the types. The first set was worth 50 points. The second set was worth 40 points. The last set was worth 30 points. I took the test, but I won't tell you what section I selected. In the next class period, she gave us back our tests. Those who chose the 50-point section were given A's. Those who chose the 40-point section were given B's. Those who chose the 30-point section were given C's. Of course, we were frustrated at how this was graded and asked her what the test's point was. She told us with a smile, "This wasn't a test of your knowledge, it was a test of your aim." She was challenging us not to aim at what we think we can handle, but to aim beyond our capacity. Having a concrete vision illustrates hidden power and abilities—aim higher.

What is vision?

Success is no surprise to visionary people. They know what they want and what is to come, determine a plan to get it, and expect the results. Vision seems elusive, yet a critical life principle. Vision is the ideal future orchestrated by God. We will never amount to much if we are satisfied with who we are today. Be irritated with what you see! God's vision defines success as radical obedience to God's unique direction for your life. Each of us has a different but important vision from God. God is less concerned with what you can accomplish for him as He is consumed with your passion for doing it. Paul was a social climber in the ranks of religious leaders. Still, his encounter with God taught him that success was not based on routine, tradition, contacts, forensic skill, or intelligence. Paul focused on the vision God had for him to be an apostle. Vision requires perseverance. Vision without determination is like an exciting chapter in an unfinished book. It does not please the audience, the author, or publisher.

If you are eager to discover God's vision so that life will become more accessible, prepare for extreme disappointment. Visions are always accompanied by anguish, confrontation, and skepticism. If you have cast the vision to others and find the approval of everyone who hears it, then it is a great plan, not a vision. It's not until you stop seeking answers that you begin to discover the answer to all of your questions. The joy of a relationship with Jesus is that he can't be seen if everything you do is finding a way to overlook him. He sees us in our most authentic state - full of sin as we show ourselves most inauthentic, and that's perfect. When you can be present in your authentic, God becomes authentic to you.

As a church leader, my purpose is to lead you into that authentic space safely. The church has coerced us to believe that being "Authentic" means being entirely against what Cultural or traditional standards are (be that "Progressive" or "Non-progressive). Seeking God's face is not something we can define; instead, it is something that occurs. You run fastest in your relationship with God when you learn to sit still and allow him to speak. Be willing to be present enough with God that he can open up the garden of your heart, weed out that which has no roots and plant that can grow. Remember, he's the artist, he's the gardener, looking to create a garden. Everything hinges on your love of God. You can't be what God needs you to be if you aren't loving God. Did you love God today? God is calling us to have our focus on the future with intentional activity in the present.

Magi and Vision

I get to preach a lot of the same Christian holidays every year. Each year I challenge myself to see a different perspective or character as I preach. Let's engage the Christmas story together. The beauty of the Christmas story is that people lived into the vision of God, not their dreams about God. It was the fulfillment of people who God gave vision to, and they trusted it. They were not comfortable with what they saw because they were looking beyond themselves. Christmas was a crazy little vision that came to pass. Isaiah 9:6 says, "Now unto us, a child is given." Isaiah is written some 600 years before the birth of Jesus. It was a vision, not a dream that was fulfilled. I want you to put yourself in the shoes of the people of Israel starting in Isaiah 7. Isaiah 7:14, *"Therefore the Lord himself will give you a sign: The virgin will conceive and give birth to a son, and will call him Immanuel."* This is the first sign in direct correlation with Matthew chapter one.

In Isaiah 7, a baby is prophesied and its fulfilled in chapter 8. We believe this is the foretelling of the coming of the Messiah Jesus. It was a tense political time in Jerusalem. Around 730 BC Assyria was busy in the north, and in Damascus they were bracing themselves for an attack. They joined forces with Judah, but King Ahaz did not want to work with the alliance because it is believed that he had already paid to be with the Assyrians. God confronts him and asks if he trusts God or the Assyrians. The affirmation that God gives is that he would not have to fight or be concerned with the battle because there will come a robust baby.

Isaiah 9:2-7, *"The people walking in darkness have seen a great light; on those living in the land of deep darkness, a light has dawned. You have enlarged the nation and increased their joy, they rejoice before you as people rejoice at the harvest, as warriors rejoice when dividing the plunder. For as in the day of Midian's defeat, you have shattered the yoke that burdens them, the bar across their shoulders, the rod of their oppressor. Every warrior's boot used in battle and every garment rolled in blood will be destined for burning, will be fuel for the fire. For us, a child is born, to us, a son is given, and the government will be on his shoulders. And he will be called:*
Wonderful Counselor, Mighty God,
Everlasting Father, Prince of Peace.
Of the greatness of his government and peace, there will be no end. He will reign on David's throne and over his kingdom, establishing and upholding it with justice and righteousness from that time on and forever. The zeal of the Lord Almighty will accomplish this."

You are going to win your battle. Why? Because your seed has to live for a kingdom more prominent than you, and that kingdom will only come because of your faithfulness. While some scholars have said that this child Josiah or Hezekiah, with a kingdom as vast and descriptive as this, it is more descriptive of Jesus than Josiah or Hezekiah. God's kingdom is not as big as your thoughts, but it is as big as God's!

That's it. God's word is that a baby will come.

Christmas is a crazy vision that came to pass. One group is being set free from Exile with a vision of an unborn Child becoming a king. Can you imagine what it was like to hear the minor prophets' sermons? Do they hear these stories about a baby, Messiah? While everyone is dying, their hope is that God will send them a baby, The Christmas story was a foolish vision. It was something that was the only hope they had that their lives would not end where they were. Jesus was prophesied in Isaiah. But, before he came there, the Magi had been watching the stars, waiting patiently for years to see exactly what was going to happen. The future was based on the alignment of stars. Their whole livelihood was based on what they saw, and Jesus came and killed their dream to give them a vision.

Matthew 2:2-12 says:

After Jesus was born in Bethlehem in Judea, during the time of King Herod, Magi[a] from the east came to Jerusalem and asked, "Where is the one who has been born King of the Jews? We saw his star when it rose and have come to worship him." When King Herod heard this, he was disturbed, and all Jerusalem with him. When he had called together all the people's chief priests and teachers of the law, he asked them where the Messiah was born. "In Bethlehem in Judea," they replied, "for this is what the prophet has written: "'But you, Bethlehem, in the land of Judah, are by no means least among the rulers of Judah; for out of you will come to a ruler who will shepherd my people Israel? Then Herod called the Magi secretly and found out from them the exact time the star had appeared. 8 He sent them to Bethlehem and said, "Go and search carefully for the child. As soon as you find him, report to me so that I too may go and worship him." After they had heard the King, they went on their way, and the star they had seen when it rose went ahead of them until it stopped over the place where the child was. When they saw the star, they were overjoyed. On coming to the house, they saw the child with his mother Mary, and they bowed down and worshiped him. Then they opened their treasures and presented him with gifts of gold, frankincense, and myrrh. And having been warned in a dream not to go back to Herod, they returned to their country by another route."

Who are these Magi? We have three men or Magi, who are often called the three wise men. They were astrologers and dreamers. They would line up the stars, and based upon the stars, they would predict the future. They would take the oral and aural stories of the culture and expect what was to come. Matthew 2 says that now these stars are lining up to predict a great dream. This is important because the last time this happened in their community was in the book of Daniel. Hananiah, Mishel, Azariah, or Shadrach, Meshach, and Abednego came to the King and told the King that they would not bow at his feet and bow Yahweh's feet.

The King was so taken aback because he knew the power of someone coming and laying prophecy at a king's feet. God was transitioning them from seeing their dream as a dream and seeing their dream as a vision. This can help you kill your last dream. Take this for consideration, I love the little kids in my church. One day our kids were drawing with some new crayons in Kids church. I asked one of the kids what they were drawing, and she responded, "I'm drawing God." I replied, "But no one knows what God looks like." They continued, "Oh, Pastor, they will know when I'm finished." People with vision know the outcome, even if no one has ever seen it before. Being a visionary is not living in today; it is living with future effort in today's murky clouds and winds.

Use your Talents daily to interact with vision

Have you ever noticed how stupid church people are? No really. They are so awesome in the world sending spell checked emails and smiling at customers. But when they arrive at church, they are the meanest, most un-proof-read people I have ever met (Insert laughter here). My church is not like this, just the churches their cousins attend. Regardless, the principle stands. Too often, we enter into spaces meant to develop us without something to be developed. Imagine a photographer going into a dark room without a photo paper to develop. The same applies when you needlessly sit on your talents in the places where it can be strengthened.

The magi were great at predicting constellations. They knew how to interpret things and created space for Jesus, but used it for their star predictions. God used what they were already talented in to show the world where Jesus was. You do not need a new gift to live into your possibility. God can and will use what you are already talented because all of us are already good at something. You have something to offer to the world to change the culture. As God addresses vision in you, God will renew your mind by showing you what you are already talented at and teach you how to use it with wisdom. Christianity is the renewal of the mind, not removal. God will renew and re-engage you so you can work strategically.

Consider this:
- What are you good at?
- What's your favorite leadership principle? What is it about that principle that stands out?
- What are you currently working on? Why that? What made that easy?
- How do you stay emotionally and intellectually fresh?
- What advice can you give me?

Leave the Dots Alone

God started with the Magi's ability to dream because they already knew how to put constellations together. In essence, they knew how to connect the dots. Do not waste away your life trying to connect the dots. I have heard of too many talented people who waste away their lives connecting their school, marriage, job, 60k pay, 80k pay, 100k pay, 200k pay, and retirement dots. As soon as a dot does not connect the way they desire, they begin to lose hope in God or begin to believe God has given up on them. You'll tap the rock like Moses and miss the promised land, you'll stay in the cave-like Elijah and lose the mantle, or you'll get insecure like Saul and miss intentional succession. Connecting the dots in your life is missing the mark in the kingdom. This is growth! A lifestyle based on you and not others!

Healthy growing people stretch beyond their social, spiritual, and physical capacities to live into the reality they know they can live in. Grow beyond your limits. Don't be like the man who bought a new boomerang and spent the rest of his life trying to throw the old one away. Metamorphosis speaks to a new way of doing things and capitalizing on a lifestyle change. Think differently and leave the dots everyone else is trying to connect alone.

Vision scares small-minded people.

While this was prophesied, the King and the community did not accept prophecy's fulfillment because it threatened their comfort. Vision will scare small-minded people, but it will bring those who are bought into God's word over your life to work with you to bring it to fulfillment. Vision scares small-minded people. But, vision pushes forward dreamers.

- Small-minded people will always try to kill vision.
- Small-minded people will always try to get rid of visionaries.
- Small-minded people will always try to work around a vision.
- Small-minded people will always try to let their insecurities ring out.
- Small-minded people will always not want to see a vision come to pass.

Be comfortable when you kill your last dream. Venture into the forest alone because other visionaries are in there watching what happens when we cut down trees.

Jesus was alone, and then he built a team.

Moses was alone, and then he built a team.

Paul was alone, and then he built a team.

There is a season of isolation before the season of impact. Light attracts bugs because it is warm. Bread attracts fish that were not there. Want to see who is with what God is doing in your life? Share your vision and watch who is there to help you follow through, and those who tell you it is too much. Passion is not transferable, but it is influential. If you burn, you ignite others. Listen to people who dream because of your vision. When people are dreaming, they are pregnant with vision.

An affirmation cannot be an altar when a revelation is your guide.

Back to affirmation again, huh? It's that important. Get off of your knees at the altar of someone else's affirmation. There is nothing someone else can give you, no matter how powerful you think they are. When you move in on your vision and not what "They" say, you will see that the altar of affirmation does not compare to the space of revelation. Your potential is not dictated by the small minds of people. But it is revealed by the mighty hand of God.

- The person may say you "Got the job," but it was God who gave it.
- The person may say you "Are it," but It was God who preordained it.
- The person may say you didn't "Get the job," but it was God who didn't allow it.

When you live into the revelation of God more than the affirmation of people, you can then begin to see how God sees your life! That's Vision. Some people feel the need to keep affirming you because they cannot make sense of your potential. Some people feel the need to make sure they can control you with their affirmation because they know that if you began to be everything God called you to be, you would take their job. The reason some people feel the need to control you with their insecurities is because they know that if you ever stepped into the reality of God on your life, you would shake their lives and their comfort.

Vision leads you to God beyond your dreams. It is a beautiful concept that will expose you to unimaginable possibilities. What have you been missing? Widen your scope and move. God is continuously speaking over each of you. It does not take an altar call or laying of hands to reveal it. The public declaration of the word over your life means you have not listened to the word of God in your private time! God is speaking. Receive what God is speaking! Just because you hear a word from God does not mean that it will come to pass immediately, but it will always come to pass.

ENDING THOUGHTS

- o   What are you good at?
- o   What's your favorite leadership principle? What is it about that principle that stands out?
- o   What are you currently working on? Why that? What made that easy?
- o   How do you stay emotionally and intellectually fresh?
- o   What advice can you give me?

SCRIPTURES:
Isaiah 9:2-7
Matthew 2:1-12

CHAPTER 7
The Death to Your Last Plan

Once I finished with my last dream I did what any person high on adrenaline would do. I wrote a vision down. I was so excited until I noticed that I had three notes left on the table. They were plans I started writing. One was for my home, another was for the church, and the last was for my own personal achievements. I thought to myself how easy it would be to simply take those plans and write a great vision and mission statement. At that moment, I realized the last funeral I needed to have. There was a reason I never followed through on those plans. Either I was not equipped to do it, or better yet, I really didn't care enough to follow through. I took those plans and had my last funeral. This chapter is different than the other chapters in that this chapter is extremely practical.

Go beyond 50%

Take a moment and think about the best planner, you know. Think hard. Think about how their plans changed the trajectory of the world and culture. Plans are great, but plans do not leave a legacy. No one remembers great planners; we remember great doers.

Doers are the ones who changed cultures, found the vaccine, led the march, and more.

The year was 2017, and I decided that I would run a half marathon, write a book, go back to school, and teach in a local university. For me, I thought they were all attainable goals. The year began and ended. I was back in school and teaching at a local college. That's it. I broke a bone in one of my feet and never got started on my book. I ended the year with 50%. While it is easy to celebrate 50%, I want you to get beyond 50%. I had terrific plans with some that fell through because of variables that I could not control, and I ended the year with items on the table.

Consider your last 365 days. Consider the items and opportunities that are still on the table. Think about what you are still thinking about and curious about. You know you are more than able to complete those tasks. Planning is great, but history books are not written with pages dedicated to planners they remember doers. Planners who are intentional to make good great, great exceptional and exceptional rememberable. Our last funeral is the ending of your last plan. You have been equipped to complete, to do, to become, to go. Planning is a beautiful start, but planning without action is a waste of your time. Quit wasting the creative possibility in your hands because you are more than able to complete every task thrown your way.

Creative Wheels and Gangs

As a child, I was taught to be "Great." I was told to dream and envision beyond what I can afford and who I am connected to. While that is all fun and dandy, it is not realistic. There is a notion of balance with faith and realism when it comes to planning. Planning often speaks to our dreams, which can be beyond us. So, we settle for what we can attain or the traps of Comparison to others who are where our dream lies. Your life is not a copy machine version of someone else's dreams. You are your indwelling of opportunity. God did not create you to recreate the wheel. God did make you to create a wheel that will be worth an attempt to be recreated.

As we begin our conversation in this chapter let me ask you:
- What is the last thing that God has challenged you to do?
- What is the last plan you started working on or writing?
- What is keeping you from completing it?
- What experiences are you creating?

There is a theory called Gang theory. Gang theory suggests that when individuals are allowed to pursue anything, they will inevitably settle. We have made our minds up before pursuit, and in the middle of our work. For example, when it comes to relationships, people know who they want, but they settle. People know the job they genuinely desire but settle for a job where they can be comfortable. And the list goes on. Gang theory says we all want "Better" we all want "Great." Still, because of our narratives or thoughts against ourselves, we decide to settle for average. Where have you settled without trying? Many of the plans we have are plans that are beyond ourselves. Plans where our finances, life, and access do not seem to match. Even though they do not match, you must not settle.

Harvest Time

One day Jesus was continuing his extraordinary leadership of His disciples. After he led them on a healing and teaching tour, he pauses and teaches them not to worship the lessons or heal but to participate. Matthew 9:35-38 says, *"Jesus went through all the towns and villages, teaching in their synagogues, proclaiming the good news of the kingdom and healing every disease and sickness. When he saw the crowds, he had compassion for them because they were harassed and helpless, like sheep without a shepherd. Then he said to his disciples, "The harvest is plentiful, but the workers are few. Ask the Lord of the harvest, therefore, to send out workers into his harvest field."*

It is such a powerful story! Jesus checks his disciples and tells them, "You are too comfortable with the people coming to me, instead of making use of your own voice." you Jesus has given them the authority to heal and to change. Yet, they waited for Jesus to do all of the work. For Jesus and His disciples, there was a harvest of souls and people that they were missing out by not capitalizing on the opportunity to do the work. There is too much-untapped opportunity left alone because of laziness in our world. People who need to hear your thoughts and Insight need the bold paint colors you bring into the world. As Jesus challenged his Disciples, I also challenge you. It is not that there are no opportunities or people; there just aren't enough workers to make the work complete.

Simply put. The disciples are more caught up in planning how to save instead of doing the saving. Jesus has healed and set free, so many people and Jesus has produced results. He looks at his disciples and tells them the crowd loves a show, but the crowd does not want to work. Then He teaches them to pray.

Where are you? Are you in the crowd amazed by how good God is? Or are you willing to activate your ability to complete?

- The promotion says you can be promoted, but you will not proofread your emails.
- Publishing says you can get the book complete, but you will not write a chapter.
- Marriage says you can get married, but you will not settle down and be vulnerable.
- Weight Loss said it is possible, but you will not eat better and balance your time.

The Lord says the harvest is there for the doers. Those who will see the harvest, seize harvest, love harvest, want a harvest, and do something with the harvest! Doing connects you back to your gift as your gift connects you back to God.

What are you, "Doing?"

You've got to be what you believe.

You've got to keep learning.

You've got to keep reading!

Give yourself an attainable do-date.

I teach at a local college. I assign a 25-page final project at the end of the semester. I polled them in the last class with a simple question, "How many days do you think it will take you to complete your final?" They wrote the minimum amount of days and the maximum amount of days. After finals were over, I reached out to them and asked how long it took them. None of them completed in the minimum, but all of them completed before the maximum. It shows that whenever we shortchange ourselves with time we lose! Impossible expectations are going to always bring you up short in the end. No one will lose if you pay off your credit cards in four years instead of two or if your complete school if five years instead of four. At the end of the day, you will have a degree and debt-free. Give yourself an attainable do-date. Think about that thing, what is an achievable do-date, and do it!

Cut your goal in half.

By no means do I want you to give up anything; I want you to remember to fight quitting. Aggressive initiatives are beautiful until they need to be pursued. It is easy to fall into the trap of settling and then stopping. When you cut your goal in half, you create a space to celebrate your progress and see your areas of weakness. So that's outlining, writing a chapter of a book, and then celebrating. That's celebrating with carrot cake and egg white's weight loss. Cut your goal in half. Many Ideas are built for a fantastic month instead of a fantastic year—plan with a purpose to do the plan.

Be what you believe

One of the worst moments of my life was when I had to admit that I was not a good basketball player. It is a day every man hates. My broken jump shot and lack of a left hand could no longer be overlooked. I also admitted that I am a terrific public speaker and networker. When I stopped doing what I knew I could not be excellent in and pursued what I knew, I could not be beaten in, everything changed. My allocated energy had a purpose. My energy was too valuable to be used on meaningless things I was never successful in. What do you know God has called you to do? What do you believe you can do? Be that! You are your responses in your worst moments of anxiety. When life brings on pressure, what comes out is your authenticity. Consider the last few moments where conflict has attacked you. What was your immediate response emotionally, physically, financially, and spiritually? Those are your core values and beliefs. Build on those and watch you lean into your belief systems that will be functional spaces to affect change.

Fall back in love with learning

In my short life, the leaders that are known are the ones who never stop learning. Life never stops teaching, so never stop learning. Learning means you are seeking to gain more Insight to make yourself unnecessary. Teachers are those who make themselves progressively unnecessary. The Shelf life of technical knowledge is 12-18 months.

Here are a couple of quick hitters you can do:

- Learn a thing
- Do a thing
- Teach a thing

When you are in a position to grow you are not in survival mode you are in accomplishment mode. Consider these questions:

- Where am I
- What am I doing
- Where do I need to go

Suppose you are still in a season of surviving. In that case, you can make the choice to move your language, your influencers, your placement from surviving to thriving. Beware of what you become in the pursuit of what you think you want. Hungry people are the ones who will always be fed. When you are hungry for ways to complete tasks, you will not let your mind lean into the frivolous. When you are focused on what matters the unnecessary does not matter. Develop your hunger to keep you on the path to do what matters. Deny yourself the thought to plan to be hungry, but to plan to finish.

What small things and distractions are around you that you are more comfortable with that keep you from doing what you are planning? When you live to have meaningful and meaning-making experiences. You change the way you budget. You change the people you hang with. You change the opportunity that comes up, because you are living to create experiences. Make the necessary endings in your life today, see the best in your days to come. Put in the work for the *YOU* that God has created.

ENDING THOUGHTS:

-What is the last thing that God has challenged you to do?
-What is the last plan you started working on or writing?
-What is keeping you from completing it?
-What experiences are you creating?

SCRIPTURES:
Matthew 9:35-38

NEXT STEPS:
Evaluate and Evolve

_____

Congratulations! You had four wonderful funerals! Maybe you have even started to engage in what you wanted to accomplish that those funerals were keeping your focus from. I am so happy for you! Now what? There is a necessity to evaluate your progress and these chapters are dedicated to evaluation.

Maybe your parents were like my parents. As I grew up they marked a wall in their home with how much I grew. They knew when I was in a growth spurt when I had leveled off and more. The best day was when I was finally taller than my father. Great times! Regardless, every few months we lined up to be measured and see how far we had grown. Because of this growth, decisions were made on whether or not to go shopping for new clothes, sports we could play, if we were tall enough to ride "That" ride. All of those things. We knew we were ready not because we felt ready, but because we measured it. As we conclude this book I want to give you a practical chapter and reflections on evaluation. A lot of plans fail because of a lack of spiritual awakenings, but because you will not measure your movement. A movement that is not measured is a movement that is marked for failure.

Every Number has a name.
Every name has a story.
Every story has a purpose.

There is a necessity to measure. Not "Measure" based on where and who you compare to but honest useful measurement based on where you are. I have seen too often measurements being used for Comparison and competition. What if you stopped comparing yourself to someone else and compared yourself to how good you could be? You have been gifted not just to accomplish a task, but you have been gifted to alter the trajectory of an entire culture. God did not give you all of God's self for you to fix a staff meeting or one situation. You have been anointed to shift cultures and atmospheres. This drastic shift in thinking moves you from particular to the universal. When we stop giving attention to the specific we can focus on the universal.

I love Nehemiah in the bible. Midway through his work we catch Nehemiah performing a period of evaluation after the wall has been built. In Chapter seven we see that Nehemiah is two and a half months on a 12-year assignment. While in Chapter 2 He vocalized that the Hand of God was good upon him (Nehemiah 2:8), in Chapter seven the hand of God did not change! He was simply two months into a 12-year assignment! Faithfulness in a one-time frame is the key to the next one (Nehemiah 2-7).

Who is in your circle?

Who you are is determined by the five people closest to you. How you understand yourself determines who is attracted to you and distracted by you. The quality of your relationships is a huge determining factor in your success. Character keeps you where your competence isn't as strong. Who are the people in your life that you are comfortable enough to influence your decision making? Life is better together.

There are four types of people in the world:
- Those who add to us
- Those who subtract from us
- Those who multiply us
- Those who divide us

We need to draw close to those who add and multiply and pull away from those who subtract and divide.

Who am I now?

As you evaluate you will see growth, I hope. Be comfortable telling yourself that you are not the same person. And that's okay! Even Nehemiah realized that God made Nehemiah stop and measure where he was before we can change a culture. God put on Nehemiah's heart and mind to count the people. Which shows us that Evaluation is necessary. Reflection turns information into Insight.

Dream in decades.
Evaluate in years.
Work in days and weeks.

Numbers shift your focus and give you a new baseline to optimize your calling. Numbers are not there to destroy you, numbers are there to give you focus! You need measurables.

Measurables are how you gauge the success of a vision. You need benchmarks so you can see where your pace and focus are. There has to be space for numbers. Because Numbers bring your fear and worry down. Numbers do not make you sit in a grey area they focus you on the black and white. Numbers organize your thoughts toward vision so you do not consider everything a failure but see the proof to ensure that what you are doing is the success you think it is!

Look at your life, where you are and what you are going... I want you to think through your numbers. Number clarifies direction not cloud direction.

So, let's talk about Numbers.

Faith
- How many scriptures do you know (Memorized)
- How many times a day do you pray?

Family
- How many people do you talk to throughout a week?
- How many people are praying for you?
- How many people do you pray for daily?
- How many people are you there for?
- How many people are there for you?

Fitness
- How much have you spent on Healthy Food?
- How much have you spent on Unhealthy food?
- How much of your week is dedicated to taking care of your body?

Finances
- How much money are you spending on your passions?
- How much have you invested in your future?
- How much money have you wasted?

These numbers tell your story. What story do your numbers tell? Instead of beating yourself up or letting your pride rise. Think like this:

- What moments do you consider wasted that are moments that you can invest?
- What investible moments do you have for your future?

Numbers are humbling, they tell you that you are not a finished product and give you Insight for the future.

Every number has a name.
Every name has a story.
Every story has a purpose.

.

EPILOGUE

My life by no means can compare to your story, and vice versa. The beautiful thing about life is that we all have unique lives to live! Each of us have been created to live life the way that God has designed it. Conformity to the Image of Christ means that some things will be shaved off and removed for God to shape us to look and be like Christ. I challenge you to be intentional with your life and with your purpose. Christ did not create you to settle, but to soar!

Take a trip somewhere and destroy some things.
Turn off the television and challenge your mind.
Pause your life and read a book and engage in Holy Scripture.

Your life is too important to live to allow anything to take your life.

Live!

I remember the day I felt led to put part of my life in writing. This book is a testament of God's grace and authority and love.

Thank you for reading!

ACKNOWLEDGMENTS

My life has been shaped by the people God has trusted me to trust!

-To my lovely, beautiful, amazing wife! She believed and believes in me when I hated and despised my own existence. I am because she has been the hands and feet of Jesus when I didn't want to talk to Jesus or care about the person I am. She's so beautiful, so powerful, and I don't even want to imagine a day without her presence.

-To my little man. Half of this book was written with him on my lap. This is for him. Your dad loves you man.

-Rev. Dr. William Buchanan. – Dr. B will always be my Pastor. I miss him dearly. Because of him I got confident in being a Pastor and a Husband. I will never ever forget him.

.

CONNECT AFTER READING

I hope you have enjoyed reading about my journey and it is inspiring your own. Allow me to join you on it and venture through the terrain of your funerals!

Go to **Jrlester.com/Necessary** and tackle the future with me

- Get small group discussion guides for your small group and/or church. These will help healthily talk about mental health.

- For Preachers, you have access to a 4 week sermon series with graphics to preach through this at your church.

- Get downloadable guides and questions that can help your journey

- Receive information and inspiration for your journey

ABOUT THE AUTHOR

Justin is a pretty average guy. He met Jesus for the first time at 12 years old, and has been meeting him ever since.

He has an extreme love for people, ministry, and coffee. For some reason Justin will not stop going to school. He attended Marquette University, Vanderbilt University earning two bachelor degrees and two master degrees while leading a few student organizations along the way. Currently he is a Doctor of Ministry Candidate at the Boston University School of Theology with a dissertation titled, "*Let's Play Church: Combating a Culture of Stagnation in Black churches through Gamification.*" Meh, Basic.

So what about the local church? Justin Loves the Local church! Justin is ordained in the baptist church. He has worked as a youth pastor, assistant Pastor, and "other-duties-assigned"-staff in churches in Wisconsin and Tennessee leading him to his current assignment as Pastor at Congdon Street Baptist Church in Providence, Rhode Island.

Outside of Pastoring, Justin is an adjunct professor at Providence College in their Black Studies Department, a Religious Life Affiliate at Brown University, and Serves on the Board of Directors for the Rhode Island State Council of Churches . Justin has an extreme love for coffee, fitness and all things Marquette Basketball and Green Bay Packers. Beyond all of this, he is working to leave a legacy the most beautiful woman in the world, His wife, Courtney Lester and his "little man" Camden.

.

Made in the USA
Columbia, SC
13 March 2023

13716825R00069